100 YEARS, 100 VOICES

100 YEARS, 100 VOICES

TEXAS TECH UNIVERSITY

EDITED BY ALIZA WONG, SEAN CUNNINGHAM, TERRY GREENBERG, AND B. LYNN WHITFIELD

WITH ALWYN BARR, PAUL CARLSON, JORGE IBER, AND MONTE MONROE

TEXAS TECH UNIVERSITY PRESS

This book is typeset in Mueso Sans. The paper used in this book meets the minimum requirements of ANSI/NISO Z39.48-1992 (R1997). ∞

Designed by Hannah Gaskamp
Cover design by Hannah Gaskamp
Centennial logo design by TRG

Library of Congress Cataloging-in-Publication Data is on file.

ISBN: 978-1-68283-155-7 (cloth)

Printed in China
22 23 24 25 26 27 28 29 30 / 9 8 7 6 5 4 3 2 1

Texas Tech University Press
Box 41037
Lubbock, Texas 79409-1037 USA
800.832.4042
ttup@ttu.edu
www.ttupress.org

Contents

BUILDING TEXAS TECH

CHAMPIONING TEXAS TECH

FIGHTING FOR TEXAS TECH

LIVING TEXAS TECH

TEACHING TEXAS TECH

The Matador Song

Fight, Matadors, for Tech!
Songs of love we'll sing to thee,
Bear our banners far and wide.
Ever to be our pride,
Fearless champions ever be.
Stand on heights of victory.
Strive for honor evermore.
Long live the Matadors!

R. C. MARSHALL, LYRICS, 1930
HARRY LEMAIRE, MUSIC, 1931

Timeline

1923

February 10: Senate Bill No. 103 (commonly referred to as the school charter) is signed by Governor Pat Neff, creating a new institution of higher learning in West Texas to be named Texas Technological College.

1924

November 11: The laying of the Administration Building cornerstone takes place before a crowd of 20,000 people. Governor Pat Neff addresses the crowd. Other speakers include Amon G. Carter, Reverend E. E. Robinson, Colonel E. O. Thompson, and Representative R. M. Chitwood.

1927

May 30: Texas Tech's first commencement ceremony takes place on Monday at 10:30 a.m. in the College Gymnasium. Mary Dale Buckner becomes the first Texas Tech student to receive a diploma after winning the drawing for which student would get the honor to walk first.

May 30: The Alumni Association is organized following the commencement ceremonies by the first twenty-six graduates.

1926

The first issue of *La Ventana* student yearbook is published.

Texas Tech receives accreditation by the Association of Texas Colleges and the Texas Education Agency (formerly State Department of Education).

October 30: The Texas Tech band becomes one of the first bands in the nation to travel to an away game. The band is in Fort Worth for Texas Tech's loss to the TCU Horned Frogs. Their trip is paid for by Will Rogers and Amon Carter.

Coach E. Y. Freeland presents the first lettermen's sweaters during convocation in the Livestock Pavilion. The sweaters are scarlet with two black outlined T's.

1925

Texas Technological College opens with four colleges: the School of Liberal Arts, the School of Household Economics (later called Home Economics), the School of Agriculture, and the School of Engineering.

September 20: Texas Tech officially opens its doors to students. The first year of classes held at Texas Tech is comprised of first- and second-year students.

October 3: The first football game takes place. Texas Tech, as the Matadors, squares off against McMurry University. The final score is a 0–0 tie.

October 3: The first issue of *The Toreador*, the college's new student newspaper, is published.

1928

May 28: Texas Tech's second commencement ceremony takes place on Monday at 10:30 a.m. in the College Gymnasium. Former Texas Governor Pat Neff gives the Baccalaureate address. The first master's degrees are awarded to three Tech students.

Texas Tech receives accreditation by the Southern Association of Colleges and Secondary Schools.

1932

The first Homecoming Parade is held.

1933

June 13: Students meet to organize the first law class in Tech history.

1934

October 1: The first men's dormitory (No. 1; later West Hall) and the first women's dormitory (Doak Hall) open.

W. B. "Dub" Rushing, a Texas Tech graduate, opens the Varsity Bookstore at 1305 College Avenue.

1936

The Board of Regents approves President Bradford Knapp's suggestion that a Division of Graduate Study be created, with the Chairman of the Graduate Committee designated as the Chairman of Graduate Study.

The Saddle Tramps, an all-male booster organization supporting men's athletics, is established by student Arch Lamb.

1940

May 8: The first annual "Texas Tech Day" is observed by chapters of the Ex-Students Association.

1939

May 29: The Board of Directors authorizes the creation of the Tech Foundation.

1938

March 2: The first Arbor Day celebration is held on the campus of Texas Technological College. The lack of trees and shrubbery caused President Knapp to proclaim that one day each spring would be dedicated to beautifying the campus. Twenty thousand trees and shrubs are planted around campus on the first Arbor Day by students, faculty, and campus organizations.

1942

The School of Business Administration is inaugurated.

1945

Tech receives accreditation by the American Association of University Women.

1946

November: Texas Tech is accepted into the American Association of Universities.

1947

Texas Tech receives accreditation by the American Association of Universities.

November 29: Dedication of the Clifford B. and Audrey Jones Stadium takes place during halftime of the Texas Tech vs. Hardin-Simmons football game.

1950

The first PhD programs are offered beginning in the 1950–1951 academic year.

Tech students hail from thirty-eight states, District of Columbia, Hawaii, and seventeen foreign countries/territories.

October 19: The formal dedication of the West Texas Museum (later Museum of Texas Tech University), with former Texas Tech president Clifford B. Jones giving the dedication and Carl Coke Rister as the guest speaker, kicks off Tech's Silver Anniversary celebrations.

November 11: Texas senator Lyndon B. Johnson is guest speaker at the dedication ceremony for Texas Tech's $4 million building program. A large silver punch bowl is presented during the football game's halftime on behalf of the Ex-Students Association in honor of the college's silver anniversary.

1952

January 1: Participating in the Sun Bowl under the first-season leadership of Head Coach DeWitt Weaver, the Red Raiders win their first bowl game. The team had also won their fourth Border Conference title in five seasons.

February 9: The Board of Directors officially designates "The Matador Song" as the school song following the recommendation of the Student Association.

The Toreador reports in February that the University of Arizona threatened to stop participating in Texas Tech athletic games unless Texas Tech changed its policy of banning African American athletes from participating in home games. Texas Tech athletic teams had played against other teams that had African American members but only at away games. In a December editorial, Associate Editor Ann Bryan praises the Board of Directors' decision to allow African Americans to participate in intercollegiate athletics and authorize the use of Jones Stadium for an all-star African American game.

1956

May 12: Texas Tech is accepted into the Southwest Conference. At 10:32 a.m., KFYO sportscaster Jack Dale makes the radio announcement from Fayetteville yelling, "Texas Tech is in the Southwest Conference!" The Victory Bells on the Tech campus begin ringing, and people gather along College Avenue to loudly celebrate in pep rally No. 1.

1955

An Oxford-style debate is held in February centering on the question of whether Texas Tech should open its doors to African American students. This type of debate allowed for audience participation. J. W. Davis and Donnie Dean are tasked with presenting the affirmative argument while Glenn Rainer and Warlick Carr represent the negative argument.

1954

January 1: Making his debut as the first official Masked Rider, Joe Kirk Fulton rides a horse onto the football field during the Gator Bowl game between Texas Tech and Auburn University. Coach DeWitt Weaver is credited with the idea of unveiling a new Texas Tech mascot during the Gator Bowl game.

November 18: Dedication ceremony is held for artist Peter Hurd's South Plains Mural in the West Texas Museum Rotunda. The classic fresco was commissioned to honor West Texas pioneers.

1960

October 15: Rededication of the newly enlarged Clifford B. and Audrey Jones Stadium takes place during halftime of the Texas Tech vs. Baylor football game. The home game is the first in Tech's first full year as a member of the Southwest Athletic Conference. The new stadium has a capacity of 41,000 seats.

1961

February 24: The men's basketball team wins the Southwest Conference title, beating out TCU 101–75.

March: Tech faculty members who were Phi Beta Kappa members form Lychnos in a bid to obtain a Phi Beta Kappa chapter at Texas Tech.

In the summer, Mrs. Lucille Sugar Graves becomes the first African American student to enroll at Texas Tech.

The Carol of Lights tradition officially begins, with student body president Bill Dean flipping on the light switch in December.

1962

October 16: KTXT-TV (later, KTTZ-TV) broadcasts its first programs as Texas Tech's non-commercial television station.

1964

Approval is received for establishing a new Law School at Texas Tech.

April: The new 400-seat University Theatre opens, with a performance of Shakespeare's *Romeo and Juliet*.

1969

May 27: Governor Preston Smith signs H. B. No. 498, authorizing Texas Tech to create a school of medicine in Lubbock to serve West Texas.

September 1: The Texas State Legislature formally approves the TTU Board of Regents name change request. Texas Technological College officially becomes Texas Tech University.

1967

March 6: First day of a campus bus route is free. Afterwards, the fare is 10 cents.

April 8: The Board of Directors approve the student body flag design, selected in an election held on February 24, as the "official flag" for Texas Technological College. The flag was designed by Jimmy Hogg, a senior engineering student.

1966

Fall: Four Texas Tech professors nicknamed "The Flying Professors" begin the first distance learning program at Texas Tech by flying weekly to the cities of Pampa, Borger, Midland, and Odessa to teach engineering classes.

International Center for Arid and Semi-Arid Land Studies (ICASALS) is founded.

1965

In the first year of Peace Corps training at Texas Tech, fifty-six volunteers undergo an eight-week intensive training program covered by an $80,000 grant. The volunteers are assigned to work in Ecuador.

October 2: The fortieth anniversary of Texas Tech's opening is celebrated all day, with hospitality registration held in the Student Union Building. The event is arranged in conjunction with the Texas Tech vs. Texas A&M evening football game. The theme for the celebration is recognizing and honoring individuals instrumental in establishing the school. The School of Engineering also hosts an open house.

1973

February 2: Groundbreaking ceremonies for the $4.8 million Library addition and the $35 million Phase I for the School of Medicine are held. Board of Regents members are in attendance at both ceremonies.

February 10: First observance of Charter Day at Texas Tech, as part of the university's semi-centennial.

1975

The official women's basketball team is formed following the enactment of Title IX with Suzie Lynch as the team's first coach.

February 27: The newly appointed Women's Athletic Council holds its first meeting.

1976

July 2: The National Ranching Heritage Center, founded in 1969 by the Ranchers Heritage Association, is dedicated.

1992

April 2: The National Park Service approves the Dairy Barn's application for registry into the National Register of Historic places.

1985

The Dairy Barn is chosen by the Texas Historical Commission as a historical landmark.

1981

December 18: The first December graduation ceremony is held, offering summer and fall graduates the opportunity to participate in a separate fall graduation ceremony rather than having to wait until the following May.

1993

The Lady Raiders win the national women's basketball championship.

Texas Senate Bill No. 254 is unanimously approved to provide for the position of Student Regent on a university's board of regents. Chad Greenfield is appointed in 1994 as the first Student Regent.

1996

The Texas Tech University System, comprised of both Texas Tech University and the Texas Tech University Health Sciences Center, is established.

August: John T. Montford is chosen to serve as the university's first chancellor. He would serve in this capacity for five years (resigning in September 2001) and oversaw a very successful capital campaign fundraising program.

2005

Starting in the fall, women begin serving in the role of Raider Red. Due to high demand and class schedules, multiple students are selected to portray the mascot. The women are selected from the membership of the High Riders and the men from the membership of the Saddle Tramps.

2006
December: Kent R. Hance is appointed chancellor of the TTU System. He would serve in this capacity until his retirement in July 2014.

2009
From 2009 to 2013, Red Raider Camp combines with New Student Orientation to become Red Raider Orientation.

2010
Chancellor Hance launches the Vision and Tradition capital campaign, which would achieve and exceed its $1 billion goal.

2012
January: The new, state-of-the-art Rawls College of Business Building officially opens for classes.

2016
April 1: Texas Tech University and Hill College (Cleburne, Texas) sign a partnership agreement allowing students who had earned an associate degree to transfer to Texas Tech to complete a bachelor's degree.

May 19: The first annual Lavender Graduation ceremony at Texas Tech, hosted by the RISE Office, celebrates the success of soon-to-be-graduating LGBTQIA students.

2014
June 15 and 17: Under Coach Tim Tadlock, the men's baseball team makes its first appearance in Omaha for the College World Series. In game 3, Tech loses 2–3 to TCU and in game 7 Tech loses 1–2 to Ole Miss.

2013
Fearless Champion succeeds Midnight Matador as the new official name of the Masked Rider's horse.

2017
September 25: Undergraduate enrollment for full-time equivalent (FTE) Hispanic students reaches 27.8 percent in the fall semester, qualifying Texas Tech to meet the minimum student enrollment requirement for status as a Hispanic Serving Institution (HSI). This status opens new funding opportunities for the university, its faculty, researchers, and students.

2018
March 23: For the first time in the men's basketball team's history, the Red Raiders advance to the Elite Eight round of the NCAA tournament.

May 10: Ribbon-cutting ceremony for the new Costa Rica campus in San Jose.

2019

April 8: The men's basketball team loses its first NCAA national championship game 77–85 against the Virginia Cavaliers. Despite the loss, the heavy media coverage of the team's strong season results in a spike of applications to the university.

May: The Texas Legislature approves funding for a new School of Veterinary Medicine.

June 7: The men's track and field team wins the national NCAA outdoor track and field championship in Austin, Texas. The achievement marks the first time a Texas Tech men's athletic team won a national championship, and only the second time any Texas Tech athletic team had won a national championship since the university's opening in 1925.

2020

March 30: Following a week of canceled classes, Texas Tech students are transitioned to virtual learning for the remainder of the semester.

May 23: Due to the COVID-19 pandemic, the university holds its first fully virtual commencement ceremony.

Fall semester classes are held both in person and virtually, as is December commencement.

2021

Raider Red takes first place at the NCA & NDA Collegiate Cheer and Dance Championship in April.

May 7: Special commencement ceremony is held for alumni who graduated in May and August 2020 and were not able to attend an in-person ceremony due to the COVID-19 pandemic.

August: The new School of Veterinary Medicine welcomes its inaugural student class.

Texas Tech marks thirteen consecutive years of enrollment growth and welcomes 40,666 students in the fall.

September 13–17: The inaugural Hispanic Serving Institution (HSI) Week is held at TTU as part of the Hispanic/Latinx Heritage Month celebratory activities.

Texas Tech launches *Evermore*, the Texas Tech University magazine.

Newsweek releases its inaugural "Best Online Learning Schools 2022" and names Texas Tech the #1 school for online education in a list of 150 institutions of higher education.

December: Texas Tech breaks ground on a $100 million Academic Sciences Building to be built in the heart of campus. The building will house teaching and laboratory space for five departments within the College of Arts & Sciences.

December 28: Texas Tech plays Mississippi State at the Liberty Bowl and trounces the Bulldogs, 34–7.

2022

January: Gordon Davis generously gifts Texas Tech University and the College of Agricultural Sciences and Natural Resources $44 million, the single largest philanthropic donation in the university's history. CASNR is renamed the Davis College in grateful recognition.

March: Mark Adams coaches the TTU Men's Basketball team to the Sweet 16.

April: The Texas Tech University School of Veterinary Medicine celebrates its grand opening after several delays because of COVID-19. Governor Abbott and several other dignitaries are present. The school's first class of students began their educational journey in fall 2021.

Texas Tech University celebrates a record number of Fulbright Student Awards, including six finalists and three semi-finalists. As well, Texas Tech University is included on the list of US colleges and universities that produced the most 2021–22 faculty Fulbright US Scholars.

Raider Red defends his national title at the National Cheerleaders Association (NCA) & National Dance Alliance (NDA) Collegiate Cheer and Dance Championships.

The Texas Tech University Pom Squad wins the International Cheer Union World Cheerleading Gold Medal in Jazz Dance, competing as Team USA as the National Premier Jazz Team.

Fall: Texas Tech University celebrates the ribbon cutting of the Black Cultural Center on campus, which honors the histories and achievements of Black students and alumni and seeks to support and sustain continued successes and more equitable and inclusive experiences for Black students.

December: Texas Tech launches its Centennial Celebration with a yearlong calendar of events that honors the past, heralds the future, and continues the commitment to academic success, creative and research excellence, athletic prowess, and outreach and engagement locally, nationally, and globally.

2023

February 10: Texas Tech celebrates its 100th birthday.

Timeline credits: Texas Tech University Southwest Collection / Special Collections Library; Texas Tech University System

Foreword

You are the first group of young men and women ever to enter the Texas Technological College. There will be many other groups, but there will never be another first group. It is a magnificent country in which our college is located. It is a region of magnificent distances, of far-flung horizons, of deep canyons, of lofty far-arching skies.

Everything that is done on these West Texas Plains ought to be on a big scale. It is a country that lends itself to bigness. It is a country that does not harmonize with things little or narrow or mean. Let us make the work of our college fit in with the scope of our country. Let our thoughts be big thoughts and broad thoughts. Let our thinking be in world-wide terms.

PRESIDENT PAUL W. HORN,
MESSAGE TO THE FACULTY, STAFF, AND STUDENTS
IN THE FIRST *LA VENTANA*

With the stroke of his pen, on February 10, 1923, Governor Pat Neff signed legislation creating the state's newest opportunity for higher education—established then as Texas Technical College—in the western half of Texas. A century later, Texas Tech University has grown from a small West Texas teaching college into a nationally prominent, Carnegie Very High Research Activity (R1) institution with a global footprint.

Over this first century, Texas Tech has become a second home for so many students and the place where they spent some of the most defining moments of their lives. Our campus was the place where young men and women grew up and began the pursuit of dreams that carried them to the pinnacle of their careers. Texas Tech was a place where they belonged, discovered their full potential, and found their voices.

The Lubbock community embraced our students from the first moment they stepped foot on our campus and inspired them to quickly adapt to the deeply held West Texas traits of grit and perseverance. While here, our students learn the value of working harder and longer and with purpose and conviction. These traits and values propel them to successful professional careers across numerous fields and industries, while others are led to answer the call to service for our country, their communities, their families, and their faith.

Texas Tech is the place where couples first meet, families are created, and a lifelong and deeply personal love affair with the university is born. This love and passion for Texas Tech is passed down to generations of Red Raiders that follow in their footsteps, maintaining a legacy of pride, education, service, and devotion.

Texas Tech has always been and will always be about its people. Pride in our school, pride in our ability to educate and serve, and pride in our focus on delivering personal one-on-one experiences is the foundation of our campus culture. Our people are our greatest value proposition, what sets us apart from every other institution of higher education in America.

Paul W. Horn, our founding president, set forth a grand vision for this university back in 1925 when he challenged us to think big and in worldwide terms. He could never have imagined that one single paragraph in that speech would inspire thousands of students, faculty, staff, and administrators to defy the odds and expectations in creating one of the largest public research universities in the nation. We overcame what many thought was impossible because we have never been afraid to think or dream big.

The next 100 years for Texas Tech will look vastly different from what either President Horn or I could ever imagine. Higher education will continue to change, and we must be adaptable and forward thinking in our approach to meet the needs of future generations of students that will come to Texas Tech looking to make their mark on the world. With an increased focus on technology and innovation, layered with critical thinking skills and our values of grit and perseverance, we can be certain that Texas Tech students will be prepared to thrive in a global twenty-first century workforce.

In *100 Years, 100 Voices*, you will see familiar names and read familiar stories of Red Raiders and their impact upon this university. Just as important, you will be introduced to unfamiliar names and unfamiliar stories of those whose impact has been equally significant. Each of them possessed a unique ability to think big, and they left a profound and indelible imprint upon this university. These 100 voices amplify the hundreds of thousands more Red Raider voices that have also defined what Texas Tech University has become. It is our hope that the 100 voices in this book will echo into the future to inspire the next century of students who will inevitably make their mark and shape our institution.

For 100 years, we have taken inspiration from the vast and majestic skies of West Texas and the leadership of those that came before us. We have thought big, and we have dreamed big. The time has now come to usher in a new era for Texas Tech, so we must rise to this moment and chart the trajectory for our next 100 years.

As we embark upon our second century, we must elevate our thinking from big to *bold*. We must work tirelessly to open our doors to those seeking knowledge and life-changing opportunity. We must be courageous in our endeavors to find creative and unique solutions to worldwide problems, while standing at the forefront of discovery and innovation. We must look beyond the horizon, always in pursuit of making the impossible . . . possible.

LAWRENCE SCHOVANEC
PRESIDENT, TEXAS TECH UNIVERSITY

Preface

There still remains the question which really arose first when we considered the question of the College-That-Is-To-Be; namely, whom do we wish to attend this institution as students?

The answer seems to me to be perfectly easy, namely—

Everybody who wishes to attend and who can profit by the instruction to be given.

It should be the policy of a college in a democracy not to build a fence around it in order to keep out folks who want to enter but rather to build steps up to it in order that those may enter who desire to do so and can profit by so doing.

FORMER TTU PRESIDENT PAUL WHITFIELD HORN
FROM TEXAS TECHNOLOGICAL COLLEGE,
"FOREWORD—THE COLLEGE THAT IS TO BE"
REPORT TO THE BOARD OF DIRECTORS, JANUARY 1925

For 100 years, Texas Tech University has been building its proverbial steps to allow access and opportunity, dreams and realities, invention and creativity to all those who would enter our doors and walk our hallways. The construction of these steps has not always been even or unchallenged or even equitable—but build them we did and build them WE ARE STILL DOING. Because ultimately, we do not seek perfection. We seek improvement. Betterment. Enlargement. Empowerment. And over a century, we have faced immense challenges: economic depression, tornadoes, droughts, world wars, segregation, pandemics. And over a century, we have overcome even more. Together. We have found a way to break into our next century. To answer the call and embrace our identity as change-makers. Because ours is that university that seeks to welcome equally the son of a farmer from Idalou, the daughter of a jazz musician from Houston, the child of an astronaut from Temple, the grandchild of a teacher from Lubbock, the great-grandchild of a migrant worker from the borderlands. Because ours is that university that, even as we respect and embrace one another's diversity of identities, experiences, expertise, and backgrounds, we come together as one nation, one Red Raider Nation. Full of possibilities. Looking beyond the horizon.

So while we celebrate the myriad voices, the hundreds, thousands, millions of voices that have helped to build this place we call Texas Tech, this place we call home, we also look forward to hearing the chorus of new singers who will belt out "The Matador Song" while cheering on our athletics teams, tears in their eyes as they sing it as our newest class members, lumps in their throat at commencement as they realize they sing it for the last time as students and for the first time as alumni.

This book barely scratches the surface of all the people—their hearts, their souls—who have given to this university, the pantheon of faculty, staff, students, alumni, community members, dreamers, artists, engineers, scientists, politicians, writers, historians, journalists, chefs, philanthropists, entrepreneurs, farmers, athletes, dancers, physicians, nurses, and so, so many more. But it is our hope that you can open the pages of this book at any point and discover a story that you may never have known or a narrative all too familiar—but it matters little because they are all tales of the Texas Tech that you love. And you will discover another little piece of yourself. Another piece of the place you call home. The place that is your alma mater. That has given you intellectual sustenance. Your greatest joys. Your enduring sadnesses. Your uncompromising failures. Your most surprising successes. Your most loyal community. Your most nostalgic memories.

And it is our hope that you are inspired to help the next century of voices find their own pages, their own words, their own book.

One hundred years, one hundred voices. Not enough to capture the immensity that spans a century of Texas Tech experiences. But enough to celebrate not just the vision but the manifestation of the College-That-Is-To-Be into the University-That-Defines-The Future.

Because . . . from here, it's possible.

ALIZA WONG, ON BEHALF OF SEAN CUNNINGHAM,
TERRY GREENBERG, AND B. LYNN WHITFIELD

100 YEARS, 100 VOICES

BUILDING

TEXAS TECH

Jim and Jere Lynn Burkhart

James (Jim) and Jere Lynn Burkhart laid the foundation, mixed the mortar, painted the walls, built the furniture, and peopled the building. Even so, the Burkharts would say that this is the house that Collin built.

Collin, the Burkharts' grandson, was diagnosed with autism at a time when little was known about Autism Spectrum Disorder (ASD). James and Jere Lynn raised Collin with love, understanding, and patience even when there were very few support structures available to them. They struggled; they were frustrated. There was so little information about autism. In fact, the term itself did not exist before 1908, and it wasn't until 1980 that the American Psychiatric Association recognized it in the Diagnostic and Statistical Manual of Mental Disorders. The connections between autism and other conditions like Asperger's and Rett did not come until 2013. For James and Jere Lynn, helping Collin meant doing research of their own, having an immensity of forbearance, and keeping the faith that they could help their grandchild.

Loving and growing with Collin resulted in the two of them wanting to make sure that other parents and guardians would be empowered with knowledge, data, techniques, and strategies.

So they decided to build a house for their own and all the other Collins in West Texas. They approached Texas Tech with the idea to establish a center focused on the study of autism that could offer support and resources to families and students. The Burkhart Center for Autism Education and Research opened in 2005 and seeks to "increase the quality of life for individuals with autism and their families by providing services, preparing educators, and conducting research." The center offers services for individuals with autism disorders, trains teachers, and conducts research on ways to improve the lived lives of people with autism. Within the center, the Transition Academy works with young adults aged 18 to 30 years diagnosed with ADS to build job and social skills that will enrich their life experience and might lead to productive, dignified employment. The Burkhart Center also houses the Connections for Academic Success and Employment (CASE) Program that offers customized support based on research and data for students with autism and other developmental disabilities to navigate college and to prepare and find employment after graduation.

Jere Lynn did not set out to become a revolutionary—she was just a grandmother who loved her grandson and wanted to make the best life possible for him and provide him with all the opportunities she could—but a revolutionary she is. For in loving her grandchild with strength and courage, she helped to build a movement to speak for people who did not have a voice; to advocate for their rights, education, and dignity; and to understand better how to empower them to possibility.

It is fitting that Jere Lynn and James would find a way to build their dream for Collin at Texas Tech because, despite the relative lack of research and resources on autism, from here, it's possible. And the house that Collin built stands strong and has already helped thousands of families, schools, scholars, and educators—not just in West Texas but across the nation—to love, support, and surround those who need it most.

Images courtesy of Texas Tech Communications and Marketing

For James and Jere Lynn, helping Collin meant doing research of their own, having an immensity of forbearance, and keeping the faith that they could help their grandchild.

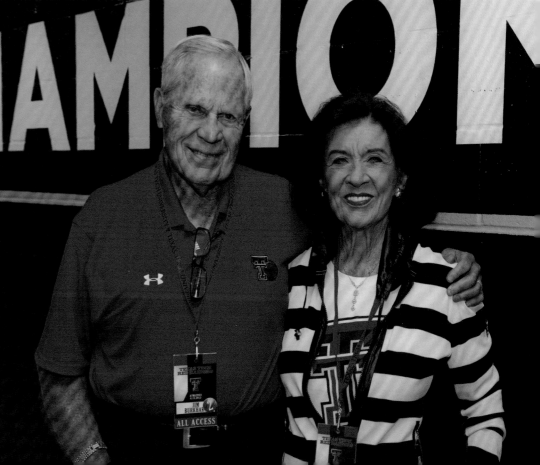

Lauro F. Cavazos

A sixth-generation Texan, Lauro F. Cavazos was born on the historic King Ranch near Kingsville, Texas, where his father was foreman of the Santa Gertrudis Division. His grandfather Gerardo Alvarez had been manager of the same division. Dr. Cavazos is a proud *Kineño*, or one of King's people, and a descendant, through Gerardo, of the legendary Francisca Alvarez, the so-called "Angel of Goliad," who saved some of Colonel William Fannin's soldiers from being massacred at Goliad Presidio during the Texas Revolution. His father was a World War I veteran, and Dr. Cavazos was a member of that vanishing cohort regarded by many Americans as the Greatest Generation, a World War II veteran.

Following his Army service, he received his BA in zoology (1949) and MA in zoology (1951), both from Texas Technological College. After receiving his PhD degree in physiology (1954) from Iowa State University, he became associate professor of anatomy at the Medical College of Virginia from 1954 to 1964, and professor, department chair, and dean of the Tufts University School of Medicine from 1964 to 1980. In 1980, he returned to his alma mater to serve as the tenth president, both of Texas Tech University and the Texas Tech University Health Sciences Center, becoming the first alumnus to do so. During his tenure, which ended in 1988, he conspicuously contributed to the university, the Lubbock community, and other communities in Texas. Counting the children of Dr. and Peggy Cavazos and various other members of the illustrious family—including US Army four-star general Richard Cavazos and Bobby Cavazos, the All-American football great from Tech—the extended family has amassed some thirty degrees from the university.

In 1988, Dr. Cavazos was approved by the US Senate to become the first Hispanic American Secretary of Education, serving under both presidents Ronald Reagan and George H. W. Bush. Indeed, he became the first Hispanic and Texas Tech alumnus to be appointed to the US cabinet. As Secretary of Education, he initiated reforms to the federal student loan programs, participated in the development of the National Education Goals, and promoted the parental right to choose the school their children attend. Dr. Cavazos targeted resources to improve opportunities for those most in need and initiated programs to combat drug and alcohol use. He provided leadership to encourage parental and community participation in education reform. Secretary Cavazos also worked at the national level to improve the education minorities receive so that they could be prepared to enter the health-care professions.

Dr. Cavazos vigorously worked in the fields of both medicine and education. He was consultant to national and international health organizations, including the World Health Organization and the Pan American Health Organization. He authored or co-authored approximately ninety publications on reproduction physiology, fine structure of cells and tissues, medical education, and general education. He and his wife, the former Peggy A. Murdock, BSN, RN, are the parents of ten children and numerous grandchildren, many of whom are Tech grads. Dr. Cavazos used to say, his family "bleeds Red and Black!" He passed away in 2022 and is sorely missed.

Dr. Cavazos was a member of that vanishing cohort regarded by many Americans as the Greatest Generation, a World War II veteran.

Gordon Davis

Gordon Davis has worn a lot of hats. He was a farm boy, a teacher, a researcher, a university professor at Texas A&M, Tennessee, and Texas Tech University, an entrepreneur, and now a philanthropist. With a $44 million gift to the newly named Gordon W. Davis College of Agricultural Sciences and Natural Resources, Gordon has become the patron who has made the largest single donation to the institution in Texas Tech history.

However, when you meet Gordon Davis, he's less likely to tell you about his successes than to recount the victories of his former students.

"It all began with potatoes," he tells us. "I coached a potato judging team."

When he was a teacher and mentoring a group of unruly boys, potatoes were cheap and easy to obtain. Thus, they became an accessible teaching tool. In instructing his students on how to judge the grade of potatoes, Gordon knew he was teaching them life skills. He was helping them to read soil, to understand peel, to examine the bumps and divots and eyes. Moreover, he was mentoring these young men on public speaking skills, giving them the confidence to address a panel of judges and experts, teaching them seriousness and professionalism. He was inspiring a competitive spirit, giving them a valuable edge.

One student in particular, Doofus—Doof for short (Gordon gave all his students nicknames)—like many of the other kids in his class just needed someone to believe in him. At six-foot-eleven, Doof had been the great hope of the basketball coach. But the young man couldn't hit a layup and proved to be much worse at basketball than he was at potato judging. When basketball didn't work out, Gordon took Doof under his wing. He teased him. He cajoled him. He gave him constructive criticism. And when he didn't perform, Gordon both castigated and consoled him. Most of all, he never gave up on him. Following Gordon's example, the rest of the students on the team didn't either. They stood up for Doofus. They cheered him on. They took him in.

Now Gordon has had numerous students who have gone on to illustrious careers, kids who earned doctorates and won numerous research awards, who got patents and published papers and made agricultural discoveries, who went on to win national titles in meat judging. With this $44 million gift, he will change even more lives and push the Davis College of Agricultural Sciences and Natural Resources to new heights, to new horizons.

Gordon remembers Doofus because in teaching him he learned an important lesson himself: by judging potatoes, the students judged themselves. And all those divots and scars and scratches weren't imperfections, they were stories. Of courage and vulnerability and strength and hope and confidence.

So years later, when Gordon, moved on from high school teaching to a university faculty position, received a phone call in his office, he was moved beyond belief. "Dr. Davis?" inquired the voice on the other end of the line. "This is Doofus. Remember me? I just wanted to let you know I'm okay. I'm married now. I have a wife. I have kids. And I'm driving a truck. I'm doing all right."

Gordon had tears in his eyes. So many accomplishments achieved: innovations and inventions; accolades and awards; publications and presentations and recognitions; students inspired through his company, CEV Multimedia (now iCEV); so much that will be done with his generosity of spirit and his enormous gift to the Davis College.

But Doof and his truck driving and his wife and kids? Worth all the potatoes in the world.

Image courtesy of Texas Tech Marketing and Communications

With a $44 million gift to the newly named Gordon W. Davis College of Agricultural Sciences and Natural Resources, Gordon Davis has become the patron who has made the largest single donation to the institution in Texas Tech history.

Marshall Clint Formby

The road Marshall Formby took from Dickens County to Lubbock to attend Texas Tech in 1928 was not the smooth four-lane divided road Highway 62/82 is today. When working on his government degree at Texas Technological College, Formby was a few decades away from his six years on the Texas Highway Commission, the last two as chairman. Formby pushed for wide highways and four-lane divided roads wherever possible across the Lone Star State. During his time on the Highway Commission, farm-to-market paved roads were accelerated, and the Texas Turnpike was built between Dallas and Fort Worth.

Formby graduated from Texas Tech in 1932 during the Depression and thrived with careers in government, law, and media. To pay for college, he washed dishes in a restaurant, did custodial work, and wrote a Texas Tech column for the *Lubbock Avalanche-Journal*. Formby became editor of *The Toreador*, the school newspaper.

After farming and running a drugstore in McAdoo after graduation, Formby became Dickens County Judge in 1936 at age 25—one of the youngest county judges in Texas. He cut property taxes and put Dickens County on a cash basis for the first time in fifteen years. Four years later he was a state senator. He spent four years with the Army Corps of Engineers in Europe during World War II.

Formby added a master's degree in journalism from the University of Texas and a law degree from Baylor. He practiced law in Plainview, which became his home. He operated the *Plainview Tribune* and the *Aspermont Star* and built a radio station network across the South Plains and Panhandle. Formby ran for governor in 1962 but lost in the Democratic primary to John Connally. Formby followed election results from a hospital where his wife Sharleen and their children were recovering from a serious auto accident.

Formby was not done with service, however. From 1967 to 1971 he was a Texas Tech regent and served as president of the then-called Ex-Student Association and the Texas Tech Foundation. He was on the Texas Higher Education Coordinating Board after his time as a regent. During his term, Formby made the recommendation for his alma mater's name change to Texas Tech University, and the board approved a veterinary school.

Formby loved Texas Tech, said his nephew, former TTU System chancellor Robert Duncan, adding the only complaint he ever heard from Formby about Tech was how he could never find a parking place. Clint Formby, nephew and business partner who also served as a Tech regent, described his uncle as a person "who swam upstream . . . and had his mind set on what he wanted to do."

Formby died in 1984, but his name lives on across West Texas: I-27 between Lubbock and Amarillo is the Marshall Formby Memorial Highway; Plainview maintains the Marshall Formby State Jail; the Southwest Collection/Special Collections at Texas Tech, where Formby's papers are housed, has an auditorium named in his honor. Formby's funeral service was held in Plainview, and he was buried in McAdoo. Mourners followed farm-to-market roads for the burial. The historical plaque at Formby's grave in McAdoo reads:

Exemplifies the hard working, never say quit character of West Texans whom he so vividly portrayed in *These Are My People* (1962). . . . Formby represented the small town, rural character of Depression-era Texas west of the one hundredth meridian, a place where it seldom rained, the wind always seemed to blow, and settlers met obstacles head on with a gritty spirit and a will to succeed.

Images courtesy of the Southwest Collection / Special Collections Library

"Formby represented the small town, rural character of Depression-era Texas west of the one hundredth meridian, a place where it seldom rained, the wind always seemed to blow, and settlers met obstacles head on with a gritty spirit and a will to succeed."

Ewing Y. Freeland

Ewing Freeland was born on January 1, 1887, in Turnersville, Texas, and played football at Vanderbilt University, graduating in 1912. He played lineman and was also a first baseman on the Commodores' baseball squad. His first head coaching job was at Daniel Baker College, whose team he guided in 1914. He moved on to Texas Christian University in 1915, and then was in charge at Austin College from 1919 through 1920. He next led Millsaps College in Mississippi in 1921.

Freeland made his mark, however, as part of the staff at Southern Methodist University. There, he served with another Vanderbilt alum, Ray Morrison. After a one-win season in 1921, the Mustangs instituted a "cooperative" coaching system, in which Morrison coached the backfield and ends while Freeland directed the lines. Uniquely, the two coaches could correct and replace players in the other's area. The setup produced a mark of 15–3–1 in 1922 and 1923. Surely a man who helped produce such gridiron success would be an ideal candidate to help establish the Tech football (and athletic) program. He commenced his duties at TTU on June 1, 1925.

The first Tech players to work under Freeland were a ragtag bunch. "Coxey's Army [unemployed protesters who marched on Washington during an economic depression in 1894] had nothing on us," he noted. More than 100 hopefuls showed up for the opportunity to represent the school. Some had played elsewhere, but the core was of players who had attended Cisco High School. Freeland fashioned a team that would eventually play under the designation of "Matadors," in keeping with the school's Spanish Renaissance–style architecture. Coach Freeland's wife is credited with suggesting this name.

The first game took place on October 3, 1925, a scoreless tie versus McMurry University, played at the South Plains Fairgrounds. The rest of the inaugural campaign went well, with Tech losing only once, in the eighth game of the year, against Howard Payne. Over the first two seasons, Tech finished with a mark of 12–2–5, including two key highlights: a 120–0 victory over Wayland Baptist College in 1925, and the first contest versus a member of the Southwest Conference (SWC), a 16–28 loss to TCU in 1926. Freeland managed to get a few other SWC schools on the schedule in 1927 and 1928, with all these games resulting in defeats.

Freeland's final two seasons at the helm resulted in a mark of 9–8–1, as well as some controversy. Given that Tech wanted to play against SWC teams, and hopefully someday join that league, Freeland used the same eligibility rules for his players as instituted by conference members. Many felt, in part, that this was one of the reasons why the team did not do as well over the last two years of Freeland's tenure. He was retained as athletic director but turned over coaching duties to Grady Higginbotham in 1929.

Coach Freeland is to be remembered for getting the Tech football program off to a positive start, with winning campaigns over the team's first three seasons. And his wife is credited with coming up with Tech's original moniker, which lasted until the mid-1930s.

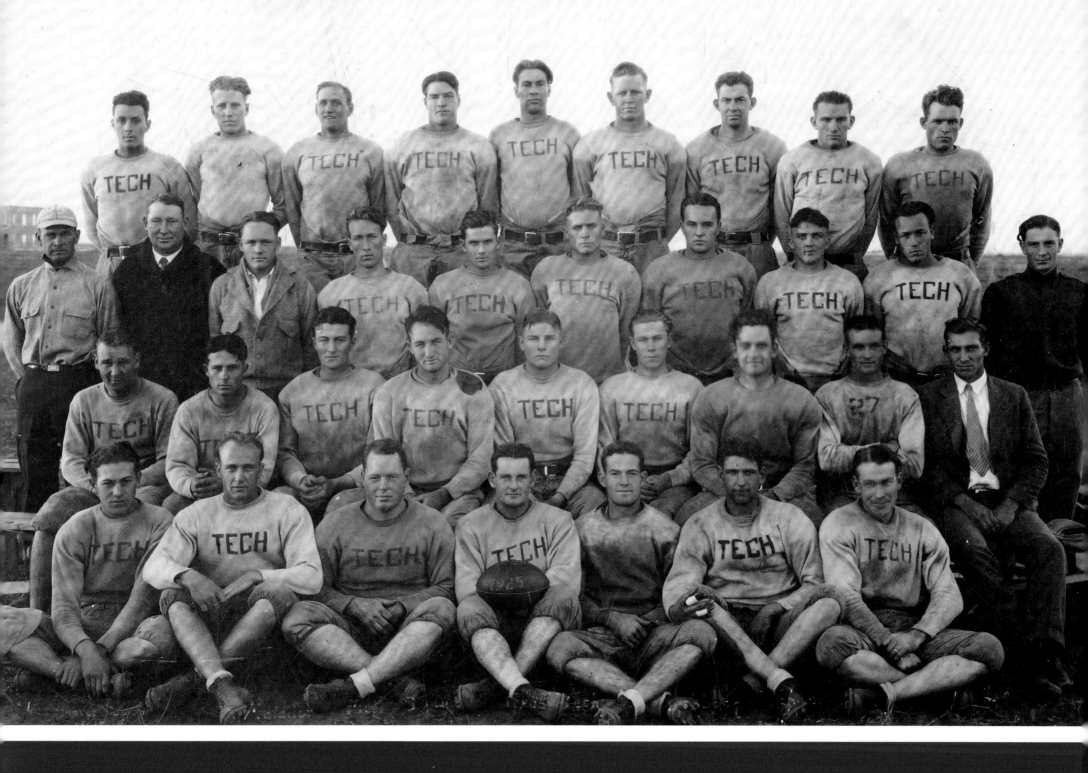

Coach Freeland is to be remembered for getting the Tech football program off to a positive start, with winning campaigns over the team's first three seasons.

Gene Hemmle

Gene Hemmle apologized to Arthur Rubinstein after a Lubbock girl asked for the latter's identification. Rubinstein—the man considered one of history's greatest pianists—was in town for a concert.

Hemmle described Rubinstein's visit during a 1973 oral history. After Hemmle's apology, he slipped into an Eastern European accent before quoting the Polish pianist's response: "Not everybody knows me, which means I should practice harder."

At a Lubbock social event to fete Rubinstein, Hemmle watched the pianist effortlessly discuss international banking with a banker, international education with Tech president E. N. Jones, and piano education with piano teachers. "He was warm and filled with humor," said Hemmle.

The same is said of Hemmle, who built what became Texas Tech's School of Music.

"He had a terrific personality," said Dick Tolley, hired by Hemmle to teach brass instruments—long before Tech had specialists in every instrument including voice. "He could go anywhere and speak. He was very popular, had a wonderful vocabulary, and didn't talk down to people. He could raise interest and, therefore, raise funds." And he was a great leader, Tolley added. "He inspired you to do things and rewarded you as best he could."

Hemmle came to Texas Tech in 1949 to chair the music department and follow President Dossie Wiggins. The two knew each other from the College of Mines and Metallurgy—now the University of Texas at El Paso. Wiggins and Hemmle shared a vision of what the then-Department of Music could be. When Hemmle arrived, he was one of three faculty members. Wiggins tripled the budget. Prof. D. O. Wylie had developed one of the best band programs in Texas, but the chorale program was weak and not part of the department, which Hemmle—a vocalist—corrected. There was no proper orchestra. A music building was built but overcrowded in two years and there were no performance facilities. Tech rented space from First Christian Church and St. Paul's on the Plains Episcopal Church—both just off campus.

"It [the music department] built like crazy," said Tolley. Texas Tech brought in educators to specialize in instruments. Scholarships increased so West Texas music talent didn't go to other schools in the state. Tech offered at the time a BS in education with a major in public school music or band. "There's no such thing as a major in band," Hemmle said during the oral history. A Bachelor of Music degree with a major in music education with emphasis on vocal or instrumental music was then created. Tech was accredited by the National Association of Schools of Music. Hemmle developed the doctoral program. He hired Paul Ellsworth, who developed Tech's orchestras. He hired Dean Killion, who became a Goin' Band legend. Texas Tech, the Lubbock Symphony Orchestra, and music programs in Lubbock schools all benefited from each other.

Four years after Hemmle retired, a recital hall opened in the School of Music named Hemmle Hall. He stayed in Lubbock, loved to paint, and was very active in the art community. Hemmle died in 1992. Tolley, Killion, Ellsworth, Tony Brittin, Gene Kinney, and Robert Deahl—all from the School of Music—served as his pallbearers on a day with a foot-deep snow. "All of us had some type of infirmity—bad back, bad leg, bad something. We lugged that casket to the gravesite from the hearse. We got it done," said Tolley. As did Hemmle, who had a vision for the fine arts overall. Years later, that vision eventually developed into the J. T. and Margaret Talkington College of Visual & Performing Arts.

Gene Hemmle built what became Texas Tech's School of Music.

William Curry Holden

Born in Limestone County in 1896, Holden lived in West Texas when his father farmed near Colorado City before the family moved to Rotan. He graduated from Rotan High School in 1914, secured a temporary teaching certificate from Stanford Junior College, and in 1920, after teaching at several public schools, enrolled at UT. After becoming head of the history department at McMurry University in Abilene and earning both a MA and PhD in history from the University of Texas, Holden was hired by the president of Texas Technological College, Paul Whitfield Horn, to be chair of the History, Anthropology, and Sociology Department.

Thus, in 1929, Holden began his long Texas Tech career of preserving the past for the future. Perhaps more than anyone during the institution's first half-century of operation, Holden helped to build a strong scholarly reputation for Texas Tech. There are, for example, his twelve books (four of them novels) dealing with the greater Southwest, and there is the wide acknowledgment in academic circles that he was the first historian to write scholarly history detailing West Texas and its social, cultural, and economic past. In the 1930s, he undertook field studies with the Yaqui Indians of Sonora, Mexico. Subsequently, he wrote four books on the Yaquis and helped to preserve their way of life. As an archaeologist, he conducted field studies among the Antelope Creek ruins in the Texas Panhandle. His early studies of this important cultural complex, which prospered from about 1200 to 1400, show how pre-horse people lived and worked in the Canadian River Valley.

Holden assumed principal responsibility for establishing four major public and research institutions at Tech. He was instrumental in building the Museum of Texas Tech University. During the Great Depression, he helped secure funding to start the historical museum in a basement headquarters and served as its director for thirty-six years. In the 1950s, he raised money for the museum's completion. He encouraged Peter Herd to construct the large mural in the museum's rotunda, and later, when the museum was to be moved, protected the priceless mural from destruction. In one of his most internationally recognizable accomplishments, Holden in the late 1930s identified the great significance of the Lubbock Lake site and encouraged archaeologists from across the nation to study its long record of occupation. Today, as the Lubbock Lake Landmark, it attracts scholars and visitors from around the globe.

Holden played a major role in founding the Southwest Collection/Special Collections Library. Recognized in 2021 as one of the major research centers for Texas and the greater Southwest, the archive regularly hosts research scholars and professional writers from America's major universities in its reading and seminar rooms as it preserves vital historical records. Holden also drove the establishment and subsequent development of the National Ranching Heritage Center, the internationally recognized outdoor ranching museum at Tech. In the aftermath of Lubbock's destructive tornado in 1970, he moved to have storm-related debris trucked to the Tech campus for use as berms to separate buildings, windmills, and other structures at the museum.

Moreover, as dean of the graduate school, Holden oversaw the early PhD program at Texas Tech. And, with others in the 1950s he encouraged the state legislature to require students at public colleges and universities to take the equivalent of a year's study in both history and political science before graduation. Holden died in 1993, and Holden Hall stands in the center of campus as a tribute and a reminder that at Tech he preserved the past for the future.

Images courtesy of the Southwest Collection / Special Collections Library

Photograph of members of an archaeological field expedition in 1934. Pictured are, from left to right: Dr. W. C. Holden; Dr. C. J. Wagner; Dr. R. A. Studthalter; Ross Edwards; Dr. Carl Coleman Seltzer (from Harvard); W. G. McMillan; Charles A. Guy; and Bennie McWilliams.

Holden Hall stands in the center of campus as a tribute to William Curry Holden and his determination to preserve the past for the future.

Kishor Mehta

Some people complain about the West Texas winds that can be annoying when they coat patios with dust. Far worse, they can also be deadly. Kishor Mehta and his Texas Tech engineering colleagues put the university at the forefront of studying how to make the world a safer place from winds that kill, injure, and damage property. Mehta and other civil engineering professors studied damage from the deadly 1970 Lubbock tornado that killed twenty-six people. They put together a report on the tornado but were surprised when learning it would cost $10,000 to print. They didn't have the money. Mehta and Joe Minor went to department chair Ernst Kiesling.

"Get them printed; I'll find the money," Mehta said he was told. He later asked Kiesling how he was able to find the money. "He said, 'They haven't asked.'"

"The report literally put us on the map," said Mehta, a Horn Professor in the Department of Civil, Environmental & Construction Engineering. The report brought national and international respect to Texas Tech. The Institute for Disaster Research was formed after the tornado and eventually became the National Wind Institute at Reese Technology Center. Mehta has served as its director. Besides a library, it houses the Boundary Layer Wind Tunnel, a tornado vortex simulator and a Pulsed Jet Wind tunnel that simulates thunderstorm downbursts.

A wall at the Lubbock Tornado Memorial honors the "five wind science pioneers who revolutionized wind sciences research and education." Jim McDonald and Richard Peterson (who was in geosciences) were the other two, along with Mehta, Minor, and Kiesling.

"We had a chemistry that was unique," said Mehta. The group met Wednesdays to share the work they were doing and decide who was going to go look at wind damage around the country and who was going to attend various conferences. "We couldn't all afford to go timewise and moneywise," said Mehta, adding that if someone were going to Washington, DC, for a meeting on civil preparedness, they would also go to the National Science Foundation and share what another team member was doing.

One of their many accomplishments was challenging the Fujita Scale, which identified tornado strength on a scale of one to five, tied to wind speeds. The wind speeds determined the rating. The team from Texas Tech had studied more than 100 storms since 1970, and their concerns about the Fujita Scale jelled when a killer tornado hit Jarrell, Texas, in 1997. Tech's engineers felt the recorded wind speeds didn't mesh with the F5 rating, said Mehta.

Those concerns led to a meeting in Dallas. Ten meteorologists were invited along with ten engineers and a few people from the insurance industry. One of the meteorologists was Greg Forbes, the Weather Channel's tornado expert, who studied with Fujita. So not everyone in the room was sold on reconsidering the Fujita Scale. What came out of the meeting was a committee of six who would look at tornado damage photos and estimate the wind speeds. They'd get their photos back with an average of the data from the other five people, then each one was asked if they wanted to change their estimate. What came out of the committee was the Enhanced Fujita Scale. It flipped the process—looking at the damage first, then calculating the wind speed.

Kishor Mehta and his Texas Tech engineering colleagues put the university at the forefront of studying how to make the world a safer place from winds that kill, injure, and damage property.

John T. and Debbie Montford

John and Debbie Montford bleed red and black. As one of the power couples of Texas Tech University, it shows in everything they have touched and transformed for the students, faculty, and staff on this campus. And just as their influence has been enormous, so is their humility. In fact, their approachability belies the importance of their gifts to this university.

One might not know immediately, for example, meeting the affable John, that he served as a highly successful criminal district attorney, fourteen years as a Texas state senator, and five years as the very first chancellor of the then-new Texas Tech University System.

Because John will more likely point at his wife as the real influencer. Debbie has in fact had a huge impact on the university as what *Texas Tech Today* described as the first "student-turned-first-lady-turned-regent" and remains one of the few women regents to serve on the board. That is why the Texas Women in Higher Education board invited her to be the keynote speaker at their annual conference. Debbie Montford continues to impact women in higher education, whether as students, faculty, staff, or administrators, in her generous and intelligent mentoring.

The Montfords have changed the landscape of Texas Tech both literally and metaphorically. Under their leadership, the campus itself became a living museum space with the Public Art Program that is funded using one percent of the estimated total cost of each new major capital project. They revived the Arbor Day celebration that brings students, faculty, and staff out each year to plant flowers and greenery not only to beautify the campus but to inspire a view of the space with new eyes and new wonder. They helped Texas Tech to create new cultural sites of belonging, spirit, and community with the United Supermarkets Arena and the Pfluger Fountain in Memorial Circle.

They also raised money to support Texas Tech, to allow TTU to continue the research enterprises of its faculty, to dream bigger in enriching the educational experiences of its students, to expand Tech's reach across the south plains, West Texas, the state, and the nation. John Montford raised $511 million in his tenure as chancellor—and 90 percent of that went to academic use. While Debbie, in the finest family tradition, graduated from Texas Tech with a degree in political science, John graduated with both his bachelor's degree and law degree from UT. John, as he likes to put it, "didn't go to Texas Tech, but he got here as quickly as possible." In his many years in the Texas Senate, where he served as chair of the finance committee and as president pro tem, with Texas Tech under his jurisdiction, he came to realize, " I have never talked to anyone who attended Texas Tech who didn't like it. So I thought I might have missed the boat by not going to Texas Tech." He made up for it by building a university system; she honored it by building more beauty.

They did it together, as they always do, with their community and friends and partners of Texas Tech. As Debbie explains, "One thing I noticed about Texas Tech: it has always kept this kind of close-family, small-town feel, wholesome, where faculty and administration seem to care about the students. . . . I know as universities get larger, sometimes that personal touch is difficult to hang on to. I think Texas Tech has tried mightily to ensure that doesn't get lost." And even as John resigned from his role as chancellor and Debbie's term as regent ended, while they are no longer in Lubbock, their hearts are still with Texas Tech.

Images courtesy of the Southwest Collection / Special Collections Library

The Montfords have changed the landscape of Texas Tech both literally and metaphorically.

Gerald Myers

Gerald Myers played basketball for Texas Tech. He earned two degrees from Texas Tech. He coached basketball at Texas Tech. And he served as director of athletics for Texas Tech. From 1955 to 2011, few individuals were more directly associated with Red Raider Nation than Gerald Myers. But in more than five decades of association with the university, one moment stands out above the rest.

March 10, 1985. Reunion Arena, Dallas. Texas Tech vs. Arkansas, with the Southwest Conference Post-Season Classic Championship on the line. The Red Raiders trailed 7–16 with 11:21 to play in the first half. They looked sloppy and outgunned by a Razorback team they had already beaten twice earlier that season en route to a regular-season conference championship. Myers's team needed a spark.

From the stands, it looked like Myers simply lost his cool. The Red Raider head coach stormed onto the court, interrupting live action to let referee Jim Harvey have it. He was clearly complaining about the officiating, but what may have seemed like an unplanned emotional outburst turned out to be one of the most strategic coaching moves in school history: technical foul. The crowd erupted. As one of his players began to pull Myers away from Harvey—worried their coach would be ejected—Myers turned around and calmly said, "Hey, I know what I'm doing."

Indeed he did. The "T"—as it became known—lit a fire under his team, not to mention the several thousand Tech fans in attendance. The Red Raiders subsequently tore off a 27–9 run to take a 7-point lead into halftime. In one of the most exciting games in conference history, Tech held on for the 67–64 win, earning a national ranking and an automatic berth to the NCAA tournament, the school's first trip to the Big Dance since 1976. "You have to credit Coach Myers with a very smart move," tourney MVP and all-time Red Raider great Bubba Jennings said after the win. "It was probably the key thing in the game for us because it switched the momentum and got us going. We decided it was time to get down to business."

Gerald Myers always got down to business. In twenty-plus seasons, Myers accumulated more wins than any head coach in the history of the men's basketball program—325, to be precise. His teams won two regular-season conference championships and three conference tournament championships; he was a five-time Southwest Conference Coach of the Year winner. He retired from coaching in 1991 to become assistant director of athletics, then took over as AD in 1996, a position he held for the next sixteen years—the longest tenure of any AD in school history. During that time, Myers supervised the school's transition to the new Big 12, managed a roughly 400% increase to the annual athletics budget, supervised more than $250 million in new constructions and facilities renovations, and radically improved graduation rates for athletes in almost every sport. And in 2001 he was almost singularly responsible for the most dramatic, nationally recognized story in school history—the hiring of former Indiana Hoosier, US Olympic head coach, and hall-of-famer, Bob Knight.

Gerald Myers always seemed to know what he was doing. And he did it very well for a very long time. It would be difficult to identify a single "Mr. Texas Tech" from the university's first century, but Gerald Myers would certainly be a candidate.

Ophelia Powell-Malone

Debates and heated conversations regarding integration of Texas Tech began as far back as 1951, when two Black airmen stationed at Reese Air Force Base sought to attend night classes at the college and were refused based on the color of their skin. Another challenge took place in 1952, when the school conceded to reverse its policy of barring African American athletes from participating in home games after the University of Arizona threatened to stop participating in Texas Tech athletic games. Educator Lucille Sugar Graves's success in gaining entry to the college in summer 1961 at long last opened the door for African American students to attend the largest state school in West Texas.

Among the first wave of African American students to enroll that fall was Ophelia Powell-Malone. Born on May 11, 1931, near Austin, Texas, she graduated from Anderson High School and studied at Huston-Tillotson College. Ophelia transferred to Texas Tech to pursue a nursing career, a goal her older brother William recalled she passionately voiced all her life. A home economics major with a concentration in home nursing and health care, Ophelia completed her student teaching requirement at Dunbar High School. In May 1964, she received a degree in home economics education, thereby making her the first African American to earn a bachelor's degree from Texas Tech. After graduation, she worked in public schools in Coldspring, Texas, and Hobbs, New Mexico. Later, she worked as a dietitian at Langston University and in nursing homes in Lubbock and Houston. Ophelia had one son, Leslie K. Malone, of Fayetteville, Arkansas. At the too-young age of 48, she passed away on September 2, 1979.

"Independent" and "resolute" were Maurice Malone's impressions of his sibling's unrelenting drive to earn a diploma from Texas Tech despite racial difficulties that still existed following the school's integration. The day Ophelia came home wearing her white nurse's uniform and proclaimed, "I am a nurse and they cannot take that away from me," was a much cherished memory of his stalwart sister. William Malone donated the first funds to establish Texas Tech student scholarships in his late sister's honor.

Mentor Tech, a division of Institutional Diversity, Equity and Community Engagement, chose Powell-Malone as one of two trailblazing individuals to honor in the naming of their program. Founded in fall 2002, Mentor Tech's mission is to enhance the quality of the educational experience for students from underrepresented populations, improve retention and graduation rates, and foster a conducive campus climate. The pilot program began with forty-six students and now accepts more than 125 new students annually. Additionally, Ophelia is recognized as a role model of resilience and achievement in the *Women Who Shaped Texas Tech* exhibit. Her portrait and biography are among the inspirational stories displayed each year in the Library's Croslin Room to coincide with the Annual Conference on the Advancement of Women sponsored by the Texas Tech Women's & Gender Studies Program.

Images courtesy of Texas Tech Communications and Marketing

Among the first wave of African American students to enroll during fall 1961 was Ophelia Powell-Malone.

Ophelia is recognized as a role model of resilience and achievement in the Women Who Shaped Texas Tech exhibit.

Janie Ramirez

Janie Ramirez walked into John Montford's office in the Texas Tech Administration Building.

"This office hasn't changed very much," she told Montford, the first chancellor of the Texas Tech University System. "You've been in here before?" he asked. "Well, yes, sir—I used to clean it," responded Ramirez, there for a job interview at her alma mater. Montford told her if he knew nothing other than that she went from cleaning toilets to getting a college education she made a good impression.

The job was to improve Texas Tech's cultural diversity. During the visit, Montford brought out a picture of the Chancellor's Ambassadors—a student service group. "What's wrong with this picture?" he asked Ramirez. "Do you really want me to tell you?" she countered. He did.

All the students were white—no students of color, she said. "Exactly," Montford said. He took her to window and gestured to the buildings and grounds beyond. "I want you to help me change the landscape of this campus," he said, "and I don't mean the trees." She did just that.

At the time, the proportion of Hispanic students at Texas Tech was about 12 percent. As the university approaches its centennial, that number has neared 30 percent, past the threshold needed to be a Hispanic Serving Institution. And Tech is one of only sixteen universities in the country to be Carnegie R1 research and Hispanic Serving institutions.

Montford left Texas Tech after five years, and Ramirez then developed Raiders Rojos, which started as a Hispanic off-shoot of the Texas Tech Alumni Association. For twenty-plus years it recruited Hispanic students through events, retained them with scholarships, celebrated their graduations, and kept them involved as alumni. Raiders Rojos has given more than $335,000 in scholarships.

Janie Landin Ramirez was born in Lamesa to migrant farm-workers. When she was twelve the family moved to Lubbock, where her dad became a janitor at Texas Tech. The summer before her senior year at Lubbock High School, Ramirez got a job as a janitor at the university. She was moved to the president's office because she could read and would understand special instructions sometimes left for the cleaning staff. Her father never went to school but understood education was the tool for his children to rise above poverty. "One of these days you're going to come to school here," he told her in Spanish. A teacher at Lubbock High and a community group helped her apply to Tech, get assistance, and register for classes.

Ramirez got a business degree and went to work. Raiders Rojos put on Back to School Fiestas that grew from 300 to 7,000 people until they stopped in 2008. They showed parents how to apply for financial aid—parents who didn't understand the process because their children were the first in their family going to college.

"They trusted us," said Ramirez, and part of the reason was that she was one of them—growing up in Lubbock's Arnett Benson neighborhood.

Four of Ramirez's children have graduated from Texas Tech, one of many examples of second- and third-generation Hispanic Texas Tech graduates over the past few decades and maybe the best measure of the success of Montford's vision and Raiders Rojos. There are several tributes in bricks and cement north of Texas Tech's Administration Building that Janie Ramirez once cleaned. One reads:

Janie Landin Ramirez
Pop—we did it

"I want you to help me change the landscape of this campus," Montford said, "and I don't mean the trees." Ramirez did just that.

Jerry Rawls

Jerry Rawls had taken out a second mortgage to build his company Finisar, which was run out of a Quonset hut with no air conditioning. He was facing a room full of 225 PhDs from companies like Hewlett-Packard, AT&T, NEC, and Europe's Marconi, angling to make a sale. He told them that his company built a faster and cheaper way to transmit data between computers. That was impossible, said one of the PhDs. Rawls told the companies they had a lot to gain if Finisar were right and offered evaluation kits so they could test it. Within a year, Silicon Valley–based Finisar Corporation became the industry standard for gigabit fiber optic communications. The company grew beyond the Quonset hut to have 14,000 employees around the world.

Rawls got an engineering degree from Texas Tech that guided him into the technology industry, but when he tells the story of winning over that roomful of skeptics, he credits his Phi Gamma Delta fraternity. "The great value of a fraternity is it helps you develop social skills," he said. Rawls learned how to recruit quality members, how to lead a project. "You learn a lot of lessons in life and business because of a fraternity. They provide peer feedback. Guys will tell you if you're getting off base," he said. Rawls said a major part of starting Finisar was being the salesman while his partner was the PhD physicist. Those sales skills blossomed in Texas Tech's Greek system.

Rawls grew up in Houston and wanted to study engineering because engineers in his neighborhood had the nicest houses. The kids who wanted to go to the University of Texas were not the people he wanted to hang out with. As for Texas A&M, which was still all guys? "I had developed an affinity for girls," said Rawls. His hometown Rice University had a respected engineering program, but Rawls' dad was a stern disciplinarian disabled from a World War II injury who needed some space, and Texas Tech was the answer.

Rawls was invited by basketball coach Gene Gibson to be a walk-on for the Red Raiders, but playing behind eventual Tech legend Dub Malaise, Rawls knew he'd never get playing time. He had fun and got involved in other ways: parties, intramural sports, student government, and Saddle Tramps. After graduating from Tech, Rawls got a master's in industrial administration from Purdue before working for Raychem in sales and marketing, then management positions.

In the late 1980s, he and his partner took a risk with Finisar. "I took a lot of risks; we were able to make our venture successful, and I made a lot of money," he said.

Texas Tech was one of the places he said thank you. His record-breaking $25 million gift created the Rawls College of Business, and another $8 million yielded the Rawls Course at Texas Tech, one of the top-ranked college golf courses in the nation. "I arrived as a 17-year-old and left at 22. I matured a lot, grew a lot, and learned how to solve problems. Texas Tech and my frat did a good job for me. They got me started," he said.

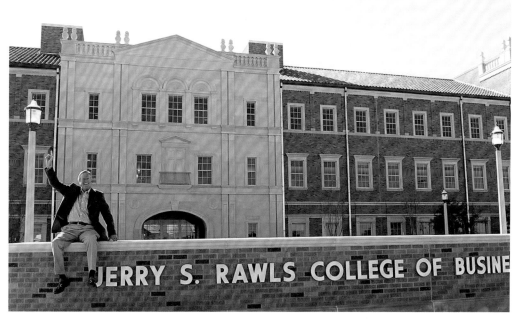

Marsha Sharp

It seems hard to imagine that Marsha Sharp was ever forced to beg someone for the right to coach basketball, but apparently that's exactly what happened in the summer of 1982 when the then-29-year-old assistant coach pleaded with her boss for a chance to lead the Lady Raiders' program.

"Please let me have this job!"

Whatever it might have lacked in evidence or reason, Sharp's simple but passionate sales pitch to Texas Tech Director of Women's Athletics Jeannine McHaney was persuasive enough. Sharp got the job, and the rest is history. The Lady Raiders went 22–9 in Sharp's inaugural season as head coach, earning the school's first-ever spot in the National Women's Invitation Tournament. A year later, the Lady Raiders improved to 23–7 and landed the school's first-ever bid to the NCAA women's tournament. Less than a decade later, it was the Sweet Sixteen. And then came 1993.

A West Texan to her core, Sharp played high school basketball in Tulia, college basketball in Plainview, and filled the 1993 Lady Raider basketball team with young women from similar places, including Brownfield (Sheryl Swoopes), Loraine (Michi Atkins), Lubbock (Janice Farris), Nazareth (Noel Johnson), and Spearman (Krista Kirkland). Under Sharp's disciplined leadership, the Lady Raiders went a remarkable 31–3 that season, earning the school's first-ever berth in the Final Four, ultimately defeating Ohio State 84–82 in one of the most exciting women's championship games of all time, in front of the first-ever sellout crowd for a women's Final Four. As hall-of-famer Nancy Lieberman described it, Sharp's Lady Raider squad "captivated the national audience because they represented everything West Texas is about."

The Lady Raiders' "underdog" championship propelled the women's game forward on a national level, but it meant even more to the West Texas community that birthed it, which explains why more than 40,000 fans decided to pack Jones Stadium on the evening of April 5, 1993, to welcome the Lady Raiders home in style. That celebration remains one of the most memorable moments in school history.

Sharp coached the Lady Raiders for twelve more seasons before retiring in 2006 with a remarkable career record of 571–189, including eight conference championships, seventeen NCAA tournament appearances, eleven trips to the Sweet Sixteen, and four trips to the Elite Eight. In 1994 she won national Coach of the Year honors, after taking an almost entirely new squad to the Sweet Sixteen. In 2003 she was inducted into the national Women's Basketball Hall of Fame. A few years later, the City of Lubbock even named its nearly $200 million east-to-west freeway in her honor.

If the story ended there, Marsha Sharp's legacy would be profound. But the story does not end there. In fact, Sharp's impact on Texas Tech and Lubbock continued throughout the first quarter of the twenty-first century, perhaps most notably through her generosity in creating the Marsha Sharp Center for Student-Athletes, which opened its doors in 2004 as one of the most innovative academic mentoring programs for college athletes in the country. She also continued to serve as one of Texas Tech's associate directors of athletics for nearly two more decades.

"The legacy a person leaves is always more important than any win/loss record," wrote Sheryl Swoopes in 2004. "Coach Sharp's shadow will always be taller than mine." High praise, indeed.

Sharp celebrating her 100th conference win, 1992.
Image courtesy of the Southwest Collection / Special Collections Library

Preston Smith

Preston Smith served in the Texas House and Senate and as lieutenant governor before becoming governor in 1969, fulfilling a dream he grasped as a young boy reading about controversial Texas Governor Jim "Pa" Ferguson. Smith was the first governor from West Texas and was credited with establishing Texas Tech's medical and law schools. He was one of thirteen children born to sharecroppers who moved to a spot between Seminole and Lamesa in 1923 when the future governor was 11 years old. The Smiths ate cottontail rabbits and Russian thistles to survive.

"If people don't think those things are delicious, they should try being hungry," Smith said decades later in an interview. Occasionally the family would make jackrabbit chili. "We learned how to make a dollar by the sweat of our brow and make it stretch as long as possible," he said.

The Smith kids walked three miles to school. When it was time for high school, Smith walked fourteen miles to Lamesa, where he stayed with a family for $2.50 a month, working at their gas station and grocery. Next was Texas Tech. Smith walked around Lubbock looking for a job and saw a sign: "A winner never quits and a quitter never wins." Shortly thereafter he got a job paying $20 a month. Struggling to pay the $25 tuition, Smith got help from the Lubbock Rotary Club.

He struggled academically his first two years but started making dean's list grades his junior year before getting a business degree. While in school, Smith got into business with a friend from the service station and eventually owned movie theaters. He also met Ima Smith—in a class with alphabetical seating—and married her in 1935. But the dream of becoming governor always lingered. If you set a goal and work for it, you can do it, he believed.

Smith was elected to the Texas House of Representatives from Lubbock in 1944. He built a legendary card file of contacts as he rose politically, learning from longtime congressman George Mahon. Smith would go into a town and visit the barber and beauty shops—dropping off emery boards, combs, matches, and pencils with his name. He'd also visit the newspaper and radio stations. When he won the 1968 governor's race, Smith didn't carry most of the state's big cities but made up the difference in smaller towns. The Goin' Band from Raiderland and the Masked Rider took part in his inaugural parade. At a luncheon, his mom was asked if she thought her son would grow up to be governor. "Only since 6th grade," she answered.

Governor Smith served two two-year terms. He started working on the medical school long before he was in statewide office. He couldn't get Tech's Board of Directors to make the formal request in 1957. Once they did, it led to 1965 legislation authorizing creation of the medical school, passing the senate 25–2. "A lead-pipe cinch," said Smith, by then lieutenant governor. But a few days later, Governor John Connally called Smith. "I'm going to have to veto that medical school," he said. "John, for gosh sakes," Smith replied, "we've been working on that since 1957 and we established a clear need," underscoring that West Texas had 118 counties without a doctor. Connally claimed he had gotten pressure from Midland–Odessa, El Paso, and Amarillo, who felt they didn't get a fair shake at landing the school. Later, Smith found out that Connally's veto was executed to pay off some political debts.

The medical school was finally approved during Smith's tenure as governor when he signed the bill creating the Texas Tech University School of Medicine on May 27, 1969.

Image courtesy of the Southwest Collection / Special Collections Library

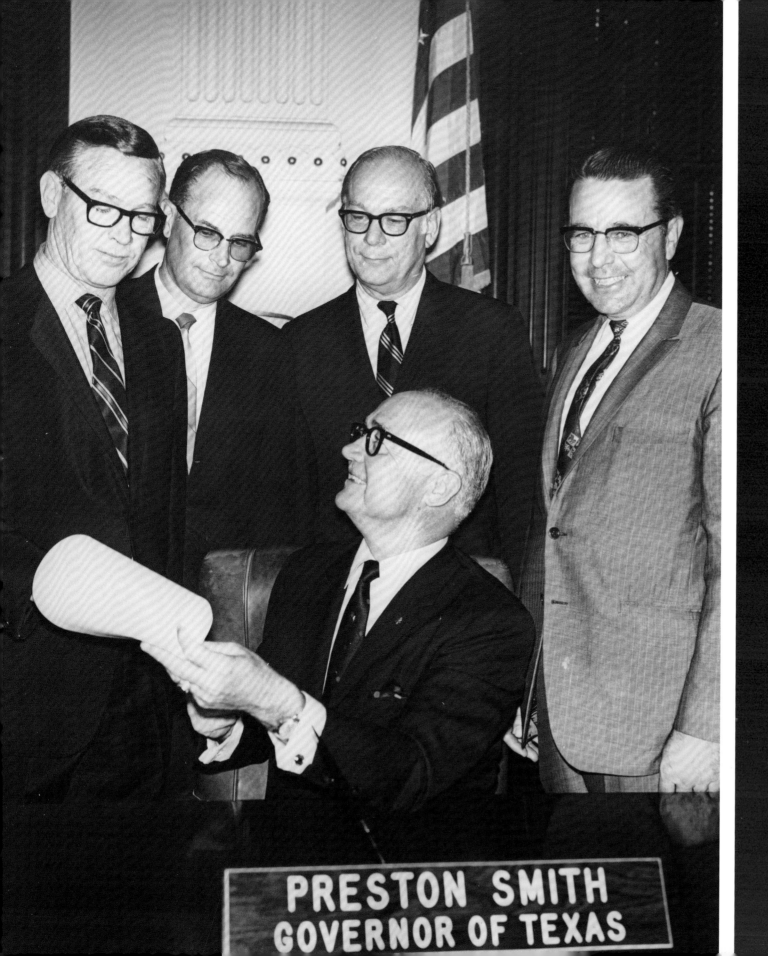

PRESTON SMITH
GOVERNOR OF TEXAS

When he won the 1968 governor's race, Smith didn't carry most of the state's big cities but made up the difference in smaller towns. At a luncheon, his mom was asked if she thought her son would grow up to be governor. "Only since 6th grade," she answered.

Trailblazers—Texas Tech School of Veterinary Medicine

Unlike many of the other projects the university has undertaken, the Texas Tech School of Veterinary Medicine faced significant opposition from every which way—financial, political, emotional. There were even moments of internal doubt as to whether Texas Tech was up to the Herculean task of creating the vet school, only the second in the entire state of Texas. And that was exactly the point. These Trailblazers knew that this dream wasn't just for Red Raiders; it wasn't even just for West Texas. This was for the entire state. This was for Global One Health. This was for all of us.

"Dream no little dreams," so many of us at Texas Tech have been challenged.

"From here, it's possible," so many of us at Texas Tech have been reminded.

Like the American folktale of the little engine, we thought we could, so we did.

The possibility was transformed into a reality by a group of people who refuse to take no for an answer, who have a response for every protestation, who countered, "But how and with what money?" with "Just you wait and see." These Trailblazers are the ones who believed in possibility even when others said, "Impossible." They believed the veterinary school into existence and made significant philanthropic commitments to an idea, a dream.

They knew that another veterinary school in the epicenter of food animal production in the world meant endless opportunities for education, economic impact, biomedical research. It also meant that the rural communities in Texas and beyond the horizon could be supported and sustained by a new corps of researchers, veterinarians, scholars who could bridge sectors and disciplines across local, regional, state, national, and international concerns.

This group of Trailblazers, many of whom were first-time donors to Texas Tech, inspired by the ambition of those who sought to be difference-makers in the university's second century, listened to the dream, refined the vision, and advocated for its completion against all the odds. They raised $90 million in eight short months. They talked to anyone who would listen about the impact the vet school would have in Amarillo, in Texas, in the United States. And they inspired others to believe in the dream.

When the inaugural class began their journey in fall 2021, they did so knowing that the Amarillo Economic Development Corporation, Mr. and Mrs. Jerry Hodge, the ASCO Foundation, Happy State Bank and Trust Company, the Bob L. Herd Foundation, the Caviness Beef Packers, Amarillo National Bank, Cactus Feeders, the Don and Sybil Harrington Foundation, Mr. and Mrs. K. C. Windham, FirstBank Southwest, N.A., the Amarillo Area Foundation, the United Family, Mr. and Mrs. Bill Gilliland, Ms. Mary T. Emeny, Mr. and Mrs. Garth P. Merrick, Yellowhouse Machinery, Co., Auto, LLP., Dr. Shannon Herrick and Mr. Jason S. Herrick, Mr. and Mrs. Michael C. Hughes, Mr. and Mrs. Blaine Roberts, Mr. and Mrs. Joe Street, Toot'n Totum Food Stores, LLC, First Capital Bank of Texas, the Josephine Anderson Charitable Trust, the Honorable Ginger P. Nelson and Mr. Kevin Nelson, the Dr. Kent Roberts and Ilene Roberts Balliett Foundation, and many donors who choose to remain anonymous, are behind them.

Images courtesy of Weston Brooks

Idris Rhea Traylor Jr.

Idris Rhea Traylor Jr. came to Lubbock in fall 1965 with a new PhD from Duke University and completed a 38-year career at Texas Tech. His academic credentials included a BA in Plan II and MA from the University of Texas at Austin; a year of study at the Sorbonne, Paris; and a Fulbright Fellowship for dissertation research at the University of Vienna, Austria, and extensive travel throughout Europe.

Dr. Traylor developed a new program in Russian and East European History at TTU and in 1967 was appointed the first deputy director and, ultimately, executive director of the International Center for Arid and Semi-Arid Land Studies. In 1988, he became the first executive director of the Office of International Affairs and, in 1997, after creation of the International Cultural Center, directed, raised funds, and designed facilities for the combined entities.

Traylor greatly increased the numbers of foreign scholars and dignitaries who came to Tech. He created the first international development projects, served on consortia boards for foreign ventures, forged international agreements with foreign organizations, serving as an officer for these entities, greatly increasing international student and faculty ties to Texas Tech, and raising millions of dollars. He helped establish the Seville, Spain campus, expanded the Study Abroad program, and created and funded Tech's K–12 international program. He worked for the US State Department in Israel and Palestine, for a US Trade Commission in Turkey, on projects in Moscow and Yugoslavia, and with the United Nations to develop ties in China. Fifty Turkish-funded graduate students attended Tech, leading to a Turkish University awarding Traylor an honorary doctorate. An award he designed for the visiting president of Chad became the official medal for Texas Tech University.

He participated in many university activities. Traylor chaired Tech's 50th Anniversary celebration; oversaw inaugurations for presidents Cecil Mackey, Lauro Cavazos, and David Schmidly; and became the "Lifetime Advisor" for the Student Senate. He founded Omicron Delta Kappa honorary society and the Foreign Service and international business fraternity Phi Delta Theta, and sponsored Mortar Board. He served as national president, a national educational foundation member, and as Tech chapter adviser for the Kappa Alpha Order for over fifty years. Traylor functioned for many national academic associations as an officer or president and worked on various other international, national, and state boards and committees. He established history department scholarships and the largest named books and historical documents collection within the Tech Libraries.

In Lubbock, he served over fifty years as trustee, board member, or president of the Museum of Texas Tech University Association and on the boards of Ballet Lubbock and the Lubbock Arts Alliance, and he sponsored Lubbock Arts Festival and Chamber of Commerce activities. He served on the City of Lubbock Appointments Advisory Committee, the Lubbock Centennial Committee, and as president and board member of Civic Lubbock, Inc. He has even received a knighthood in a sovereign Order. As a global citizen, Dr. Traylor travelled to over eighty countries and is considered among the most erudite and interesting individuals of both the Texas Tech and Lubbock communities.

Traylor (left) and Thadis Wayne Box (right) with publications and documents related to the International Center for Arid and Semiarid Land Studies (ICASALS). Image courtesy of the Southwest Collection / Special Collections Library

Elo Urbanovsky

Charles Eatherly didn't know it all those years ago, but Elo Urbanovsky's tough love prepped him for the real world of park management. Eatherly and other Texas Tech students learned to put tracing paper over their project drawings. Urbanovsky would mark them with a grease pencil, saying: "That's not bad, but I've got another idea." Another time he told students to prepare a 30-minute presentation, then, just before, ordered them to cut it to five.

The World War II Navy veteran could swear like, well, a Navy veteran, adding to the intimidation. Eatherly and other students struggled not to take the approach personally. Years later, after they had real jobs working with government agencies and businesses, they realized Urbanovsky was setting them up for success in a world where feedback from elected officials could be brutal and you're rarely given the time you'd like to share a plan.

Urbanovsky came to Texas Tech in 1949 to teach and help develop the campus with his skills as a landscape architect. The Department of Park Administration and Landscape Architecture was established under his leadership. His influence on the campus and students was huge, and his well-known big red Ford LTD was recognized all over campus. One of his first tasks was to place the new statue of Will Rogers riding Soapsuds in 1950. The original idea was to point it west near the campus entrance, with Rogers riding into the sunset. But the horse's rear end would be pointed toward downtown. It was moved to Memorial Circle—Soapsuds' posterior shifted 23 degrees southeast—pointing right at College Station. Urbanovsky believed in environmental design—seeing what you want to save on a property before creating a plan. He preferred living things to buildings, which he saw as a necessary evil. He thought it was important to wait to put in sidewalks after a building was finished until he saw where students walked. Importantly, he shaped the Tech campus to replicate the wide-open feeling of West Texas.

His impact beyond Texas Tech was equally impressive, as he worked on many projects across the country. Urbanovsky collaborated often with Lady Bird Johnson. They were such good friends, he called her "Bird" and the first lady called him "my dear friend, Elo." Urbanovsky and his students made presentations to Governor John Connally and Lieutenant Governor Preston Smith—a Red Raider—on what Texas state parks could be, which led to improvements. His involvement with various professional organizations brought parks professionals to Lubbock to work with students. Those connections were a pipeline for students to find internships and jobs. Urbanovsky helped form the Southwest Park and Recreation Training Institute.

As tough as Urbanovsky could be while getting students educated, he was supportive to former students. Eatherly called Urbanovsky after he lost a job. "Well, damn it, if they don't appreciate the work you're doing, somebody else will," Urbanovsky told him. It revived Eatherly's spirits and he went on to a successful career.

Among countless honors, Urbanovsky was one of the first Horn Professors in 1967, was given the Pro Ecclesia et Pontifice decoration by Pope John XXIII, and the park east of United Supermarkets Arena is named for him. The park was dedicated in 1993, five years after Urbanovsky died at 80. After his death, a piece in the *Lubbock Avalanche-Journal* said Urbanovsky jealously guarded every inch of university property and went on to say, "For so long as there is a Texas Tech University campus sprouting trees and shrubbery in an eye-appealing landscape, [Urbanovsky] will be immortal."

From press release accompanying photo: "HORN PROFESSORS NAMED — Four Texas Tech professors were awarded Horn Professorships Saturday (June 3) by the university's Board of Directors. The four are the first to be named to the professorships which were created by the Board in 1966 in honor of Tech's first president, Paul W. Horn. Selected were, left to right, Dr. Ernest Wallace, Dr. F. Alton Wade, Elo J. Urbanovsky and Dr. Carl Hammer."

Urbanovsky shaped the Tech campus to replicate the wide-open feeling of West Texas.

William Ward Watkin

In 1541, conquistador Francisco Vázquez de Coronado's expedition camped on what became known as the South Plains about fifty miles from the future home of Texas Tech University. Coronado was from Salamanca, Spain, a country with wide swaths of land that look like parts of West Texas. Centuries later, parts of Texas Tech's Chemistry building—one of the original campus buildings—resembled the elegant Palacio de Monterrey in Salamanca.

The Administration Building's façade was based on that of the Colegio Mayor de San Ildefonso, centerpiece of the University of Alcalá de Henares, northeast of Madrid, founded in 1508—long before there were any universities in Texas.

Thanks to William Ward Watkin, Texas Tech has an architectural kinship with sixteenth-century Spain, which it lost and regained, creating beautiful buildings that celebrate historic Spanish influence. American universities used many neoclassical and revivalist architectural styles: Beaux-Arts classical—Columbia University; Neo-Georgian—Johns Hopkins University; Neo-Gothic—University of Chicago and Princeton University; Romanesque revival—UCLA; Neo-Byzantine—Rice University's original administration building.

But Pennsylvania-born Watkin, a Houston architect, chose a style from the sixteenth-century Spanish Renaissance when he started designing Texas Technological College in the 1920s.

Watkin had worked on plans for what is now Rice University and founded its architecture department in 1912. Watkin's mentor Ralph Cram had discovered traditional Spanish architecture during a long trip to Spain and Europe. Watkin had not visited Spain before he started work on Tech's first buildings and campus plan. He leaned on two books by American writers: Andrew Prentice's *Renaissance Architecture and Ornament in Spain* (1888) and Arthur Byne's *Spanish Architecture of the Sixteenth Century* (1917). The specific style Watkin used was Plateresque. It was one of four distinctive phases of the Spanish Renaissance named for the style's ornamental resemblance to Spanish silver jewelry: *plata*.

Watkin worked closely with Paul Horn, Tech's first president, and Amon Carter, Tech's board chair. His influence didn't last, however. He had to leave the project because of a family emergency. His plan was never finished—like his great commencement hall, called either the Hall of Texas or Alamo Commencement Hall. Military barracks took the place of Watkin's buildings. Structures popped up in a more modern, institutional style called—aptly—Brutalism.

There were even plans championed by college librarian R. C. Janeway and *Lubbock Avalanche-Journal* editor Charles A. Guy to put a new library in the middle of Memorial Circle. Nolan Barrick—who became the campus architect and head of the Architecture Department—helped shoot down that idea. Watkin was Barrick's mentor—and father of Barrick's wife Rosemary. Barrick studied under Watkin at Rice and then came to Tech the year after Watkin passed away in 1952.

It took a while, but in the 1990s, Texas Tech joined a new sports conference, created a university system, and saw fundraising dramatically improve. And it rediscovered its "SpanRen" heritage. United Supermarkets Arena, its next-door neighbor the Dustin R. Womble Basketball Center, the Kent Hance Chapel, the Rawls College of Business, the west and east side expansion to Jones AT&T Stadium, and many others proudly display William Ward Watkin's vision born half a millennium ago in Spain.

Bottom left portrait courtesy of Rice University Digital Scholarship Archive.
Top left and bottom right images courtesy of the Southwest Collection /
Special Collections Library

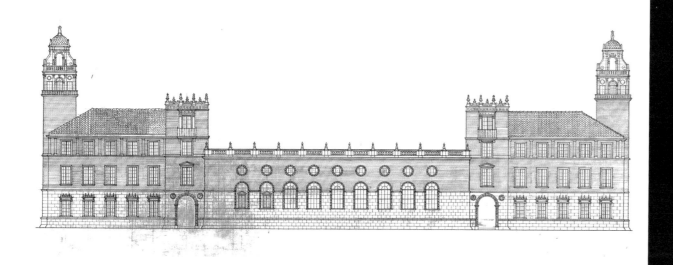

Thanks to William Ward Watkin, Texas Tech has an architectural kinship with sixteenth-century Spain.

Edward E. Whitacre Jr.

One of Ed Whitacre's AT&T colleagues came to see him after meeting with Apple's Steve Jobs.

Jobs had displayed a small phone with applications that set the foundation for the modern smartphone—elevating it above flip phones of the time. AT&T's network could partner with the new iPhone, but it would be a huge investment. CEO Whitacre later said it was as close as he ever came to betting AT&T's financial future. But AT&T's network, its people to run it, and Jobs' vision for a personal communications device seemed like a good bet. They signed an exclusive five-year deal. Smart bet.

Since graduating from Texas Tech in 1964 with an industrial engineering degree, Whitacre built a reputation as a smart, effective boss—first leading AT&T and later bringing General Motors back from bankruptcy. Along that journey, he's served and been very generous to his alma mater:

- In 2008, AT&T Inc. contributed $25 million to Texas Tech University in honor of the company's former chairman and CEO, Edward E. Whitacre Jr., alumnus and former regent. Texas Tech named the College of Engineering the Edward E. Whitacre Jr. College of Engineering in recognition of this gift and of all that Ed Whitacre has done for the university and the nation.

- Whitacre donated $8 million for the Ed Whitacre Center for Athletic Administration, which cleared the way for the Dustin R. Womble Football Center to start construction in 2022.

- He facilitated a $20 million gift for renovations at Jones AT&T Stadium and $14 million from the SBC Foundation for endowed scholarships.

- He's served on the Board of Regents and chaired Texas Tech's Horizon Fundraising Campaign from 1996 to 2001.

After graduating from Ennis High School, just south of Dallas, Whitacre spent a year at the University of Texas at Arlington before coming to Lubbock to study engineering. At the end of one semester, one of Whitacre's Delta Tau Delta brothers asked him to give his sister a ride home to Fort Worth. He picked up the girl, named Linda; got acquainted on the drive; and married her a few years later.

Whitacre had various jobs to help pay for college. The summer before his senior year he got a gig as a Southwestern Bell lineman doing grunt work. After graduation, Whitacre got into the company's Junior Executive Program and eventually rose to CEO. Whitacre changed the named to SBC Communications, because he wanted the company to be nationwide and Southwestern implied a limited footprint.

SBC bought AT&T, and the merged company was now AT&T, an international enterprise. One of Whitacre's corporate highlights was traveling to South Africa to talk with President Nelson Mandela about the country's phone company. Whitacre was also on the cutting edge of putting women in leadership roles and on corporate boards.

A few years after retiring from AT&T, Whitacre got a call from the Obama White House, asking if he would help General Motors as a service to his country. as a service for his country. Whitacre took what he called a complicated, confused, bureaucratic company without a lot of responsibility at any level and returned it to profitability. GM had a massive policy manual Whitacre ignored and told people to focus on this statement: design, build, and sell the world's best vehicles. GM was called impossible to fix. "It was very fixable," said Whitacre. On a visit back to Lubbock, he dropped in unannounced at the Alderson Cadillac dealership—a GM vehicle—and teased them about also selling Lexuses next-door. He still drives a Caddy.

Images courtesy of the Southwest Collection / Special Collections Library

Whitacre built a reputation as a smart, effective boss—first leading AT&T and later bringing General Motors back from bankruptcy.

CHAMPIONING

TEXAS TECH

Dick and Martha Brooks

Dick Brooks grew up in Slaton, Texas. When it was time for him to go to college, he chose Texas Tech University, pursuing a degree in electrical engineering. With the support of his wife, Martha, Dick worked full time at the Santa Fe Railroad to pay his tuition and provide for his young family.

When he graduated in 1961, he took a job with West Texas Utilities, where he quickly was moved into supervisory and executive engineering positions. He was promoted to vice president of customer services by 1980. In 1982, he took a position as vice president of engineering with Central Power and Light Company, where he worked his way up to the highest leadership position, president and chief executive officer. In 1987, Dick became the executive vice president of Central and South West Corporation and oversaw the operations of the conglomerate's four electric utility companies.

His reach extends far beyond his employment—because of his expertise, experience, and largesse, Dick Brooks served as chair of the Electric Reliability Council of Texas and as president of the Texas Council on Economic Education. He served on the Industrial Advisory Committee for the TTU Department of Electrical Engineering. He was a member of the Board of Trustees of the North American Electric Reliability Council and the executive boards of the Texas Association of Taxpayers, the Texas Research League, and the Texas State Chamber of Commerce. He also served on the board of directors for Transok, Inc., Central and South West Services, Inc., CSW Energy, Inc., CSW Financial, Inc., and CSW Credit, Inc.

He also understood that to give back meant to be a member of his community. He did not shirk that responsibility—in fact, he and Martha embraced it. Even as Martha undertook the care of the many high school students she mentored during her tenure as a high school principal, she and Dick filled every other waking moment by living a life of giving. They are active in church and community activities, including membership in the One Hundred Club of Corpus Christi and Acton Baptist Church and as strong supporters of the Coastal Bend United Way and the Dallas Circle Ten Boy Scouts.

In addition, Dick served as a member of the Texas Tech University System Board of Regents as a proud alumnus and difference maker—recognized as both a Distinguished Engineer and Distinguished Alumnus—who advocated for faculty, staff, and students. And on October 22, 2004, Texas Tech University announced the creation of the E. R. "Dick" and Martha Brooks Endowed Professorship in the Department of Mathematics and Statistics, the first endowed professorship of its kind in math. The Brooks' contribution was matched by the Regents Faculty Endowment Program and was part of Texas Tech's Path to Preeminence effort to enhance recruitment and retention of distinguished faculty.

The endowment allowed the department to attract a nationally recognized scholar with significant research efforts but who also enhanced the educational experience of students in mathematics and statistics. Dr. Magda Toda, chair of Mathematics and Statistics, noted the Brooks' kindness, humility, and generosity, adding, "They have a great sense of humor and are always optimistic, which makes them great role models for the faculty and students. The world needs more like them!"

As Dick explained, "Martha and I are dedicated supporters of Texas Tech, and this gift provides an opportunity for us to give something back to the university that opened many doors for us. The Department of Mathematics and Statistics supports a wide range of disciplines, from engineering to science to business, all fields that have been important in my career."

Images courtesy of Dick and Martha Brooks

Dick Brooks understood that to give back meant to be a member of his community. He did not shirk that responsibility—in fact, he and Martha embraced it.

J. Fred Bucy Jr.

At age twelve, Tahoka native J. Fred Bucy Jr. worked in a local drugstore as a soda jerk where he met nine-year-old Odetta Greer. It was 1940, and he charmed her by selling her a double-dip ice-cream cone for half the price at nine cents. The chance meeting sparked a friendship that led to marriage six years later. The happy young couple supported themselves financially through farming. Bucy, an avid reader, ultimately decided to pursue a career in engineering rather than farming. He enrolled in Texas Tech University in the late 1940s. In 1951, he earned a BS degree in engineering physics then relocated to Austin with his wife and first child, Fred Bucy III, to work as an associate research physicist in the Department of Defense Applied Research Laboratories at The University of Texas. Odetta also attended UT; daughter Roxanne was born during this time.

After receiving his MS degree in physics in 1952, Bucy joined Texas Instruments (TI) in Dallas in 1953 to work in the Central Research Labs applying new technology in development of a processor for interpreting geophysical data in oilfields of notable size around the world. A second daughter, Diane, was born after Bucy transferred to TI's Houston office. His focus on applying digital technology toward improving accuracy of oil and gas exploration resulted in the 1958 market introduction of the first solid state seismic system. Bucy returned to Dallas in 1963 and, by 1967, was heading up TI's Semiconductor-Components Division and its international manufacturing operations. Through the course of his 32-year association with TI, Bucy attained a variety of administrative and leadership roles, including president in 1976 and chief executive officer in 1984. He retired in May 1985.

His achievements as an engineer were a great source of pride for Bucy. As well as authoring and co-authoring a number of noteworthy patents, he was a fellow of the Institute of Electrical and Electronics Engineers, a trustee of the Southwest Research Institute, and a member of the National Academy of Engineering and the Defense Science Board of the Department of Defense.

A lifelong and rewarding relationship with his alma mater, which spanned more than four decades, was another source of pride for Bucy. From 1973 to 1991, he served three six-year terms as a member of the Texas Tech Board of Regents, making him the second-longest-serving regent in the school's history. As a regent, he served in the capacity of chair and vice chair and helped shape the early development of the Texas Tech University Health Sciences Center. In 1972, the College of Engineering recognized his contributions to the profession with the honorary title of Distinguished Engineer. The university awarded him an honorary Doctor of Science degree in 1994. In kind, the Bucys established the Bucy Graduate Scholarships in Applied Physics, the Bucy Undergraduate Scholarships in Physics, and the Bucy Endowed Chair in Physics.

J. Fred Bucy peacefully passed away in his sleep on May 20, 2021.

Bucy (left) and B. J. Pevehouse, then Chair of the Board of Regents.
Image courtesy of the Southwest Collection / Special Collections Library

Bob Bullock

The story's been told how Bob Bullock—the powerful late Texas lieutenant governor—called representatives from the University of Texas and Texas A&M University to a meeting in his office in the mid-1990s. The Longhorns and Aggies wanted to leave the Southwest Conference. That was fine with Bullock—if they took Texas Tech and Baylor with them. Also in the room were John Montford, head of the Texas Senate Appropriations Committee, and Rob Junell, head of the Texas House Appropriations Committee.

Junell was a Red Raider and Montford—even though he went to the University of Texas—represented Lubbock and West Texas. Bullock had attended both Texas Tech and Baylor, and Governor Ann Richards was a Baylor Bear. Bullock made it clear there'd be financial hell to pay if UT and A&M didn't play ball, and he knew how to use power to get what he wanted. The story of how he got that power started a few decades earlier and was connected to former Governor Preston Smith—also a Red Raider—even if Smith didn't know about it for a while.

Bullock won a seat in the Texas House of Representatives in the late 1950s after his graduation from college. Almost a decade later he was looking for lobbying work in Austin. Meanwhile, Smith was running for governor after serving as lieutenant governor for six years. One of Smith's trusted advisers was East Texan Ottis Lock, who got to know him in the legislature. The campaign was not doing well, so Lock and other members of Smith's "kitchen cabinet" hired Bullock to run the campaign—without telling Smith.

Bullock turned things around and eventually Smith was told. Smith was elected governor and Bullock became his appointments secretary, making recommendations on who should be appointed to state boards and commissions.

Bullock then became Texas secretary of state. His next step thereafter was comptroller, which could be a sleepy job—but not under Bullock. The lieutenant governor and speaker of the House would tell a weak comptroller to provide a revenue estimate fitting their budget needs. Bullock got concessions from the legislature to give them the numbers they wanted. Bullock was also not afraid to use the comptroller's audit arm to make life uncomfortable for opponents with what was known as a "proctological exam."

By the time he became lieutenant governor, Bullock was a political force who got what he wanted by knowing who to talk to and how to motivate them. He worked with governors Ann Richards and George W. Bush, who were from different political parties. Ottis Lock's son, Ben, worked for Bullock when he was comptroller and, ironically, ended up as secretary for the Texas Tech University System Board of Regents a couple of years after Bullock had that meeting leading to Tech and Baylor joining the Big 12 Conference.

"More often than not, what he wanted was something good for the state of Texas and good for the people of Texas. Sometimes it was good for Bob Bullock, too," said Lock.

Even though Bullock had ties to Texas Tech and Baylor, he didn't go around flashing Guns Up or Baylor's Sic 'Em bear claw. But the two schools once took care of him, and when he could help them, he did. So when Bullock called that meeting in the mid-1990s to tell the Longhorns and Aggies what to do, he'd amassed a level of power the two schools could not ignore, and the benefit to Texas Tech became immense.

Left: Opening day of the 75th Legislature - Bullock and George W. Bush sitting on the Senate Rostrum, January 14, 1997. Image courtesy of the Bullock Archive at Baylor University, Waco, TX
Right: Image courtesy of Texas Senate Media

By the time he became lieutenant governor, Bullock was a political force who got what he wanted by knowing who to talk to and how to motivate them.

Amon G. Carter

Amon Carter left home at thirteen, never graduated from high school or attended college, but in the mythic Horatio Alger tradition became a Fort Worth multimillionaire newspaper publisher, radio and television mogul, and highly energetic advocate of all things related to West Texas. Indeed, from his beloved Fort Worth base, Carter conquered West Texas—at least in print. The *Amarillo Globe* reported in 1936 that "West Texas is bound on the north by Colorado and Oklahoma, on the west by New Mexico, on the south by Mexico and on the east by Amon Carter."

Born in Crafton in Wise County, little Amon, his mother said of him, "is the worst rounder I ever saw." She died in 1892, and his father shortly thereafter remarried—unfortunately to a woman with whom Carter clashed. Carter left home, went to Bowie, scrambled for a living, and after hard work and some timely breaks became a highly successful national salesman for a Chicago-based picture-framing company.

Carter returned to Texas in 1904 and invested in the *Fort Worth Star*, a new city newspaper. Five years later he combined his paper with a rival to bring out the *Fort Worth Star-Telegram*, for a time in the 1920s a newspaper with the largest circulation in the South.

Carter used the paper and later his radio station to promote Fort Worth and West Texas. Flamboyant and colorful, he attracted attention to himself, his newspaper, and his city. He "invented the cowboy," it was said of him, and he encouraged the idea that Fort Worth was "where the West began."

As much as anyone, Carter persuaded the state legislature and Governor Pat Neff to support a new "scientific" university in West Texas. Through the *Star-Telegram*, he pushed for such a college, lobbied the legislature and the governor for it, and with the help of other West Texans, including Lubbock's William Bledsoe and Slaton's Ray Alvin Baldwin, in February 1923 helped to get the school, Texas Technological College, established. In August, a special committee chose Lubbock for its location.

For Carter's efforts in helping to get Tech established, Governor Neff appointed him to the first board of trustees, and its members voted him chairman of their group. In that role, Carter was instrumental in selecting Paul Whitfield Horn as Tech's first president, encouraged enrollment at the institution (enrollment that reached over 1,000 students in its first term, fall 1925), and continued through his time on the board to endorse and promote Texas Tech.

Carter's many close friends included American celebrities. One of them was Will Rogers, humorist and national political wit, who was also a cowboy from Oklahoma. To honor the memory of his good friend, Carter commissioned Electra Waggoner Biggs to sculpt the Rogers and Soapsuds statue near Tech's Memorial Circle. Carter said, "This statue will fit into the traditions and scenery of our great western country." Tech dedicated the 9-foot-eleven-inch, 3,200-pound statue on February 16, 1950. The marker at its base reads: "Loveable Old Will Rogers on his favorite horse 'Soapsuds' riding into the western sunset."

Amon Carter was a fascinating character who embraced his buffoonish cowboy persona. He made fun of society mavens and spoofed intellectuals. He did not read books until the last two years of his life. But he loved and heartily championed Texas Technological College, a school he saw as important in his efforts to "conquer West Texas." For his continuing support, Texas Tech in 1953 awarded him an honorary doctorate and in the 2010s named the Broadway entrance to the university the Amon G. Carter Plaza.

Image courtesy of the Southwest Collection / Special Collections Library

Portrait of the first Texas Tech Board of Directors at their October 1929 meeting after Secretary Gaston came to Texas Tech. Pictured are: Amon G. Carter, President Paul Whitfield Horn, Mrs. F. N. Drane, Houston Harte, John W. Carpenter, Clifford B. Jones, Roscoe Wilson, Bob Underwood, Riley Strickland, W. T. Gaston, Frank Clarity, and Thomas Johnson.

Don, Kay, and Clay Cash

Don, Kay, and Clay Cash were never far from Texas Tech even when far away from the 806 area code. Don and Kay came to the university in the 1960s from the West Texas towns of McLean and Friona. They learned and made lifelong friends. Kay became Miss Lubbock.

After graduating—his degree in industrial engineering and hers in elementary education—they moved a lot as Don rose through the energy industry. Fort Worth . . . Denver . . . Chicago . . . Oklahoma City . . . before finally landing in Salt Lake City where Don became chairman and CEO of Questar. Kay taught school but used to joke she was a professional packer and mover.

Their son Clay was born in 1973. He got a degree in business administration in management from Texas Tech in 1997. Like his dad, Clay ended up in the energy industry, working his way up to vice president of Atmos Energy. He started at the bottom, digging ditches, and also moved a lot. Lubbock . . . Dallas . . . Lubbock . . . Kentucky . . . Lubbock . . . Midland . . . back to Dallas before retiring so he could be closer to his folks in the Hub City, where his parents had retired.

"I'm not a Dallas guy," he said, tired of years driving on the North Dallas Tollway. "I was always a West Texas guy. It's also a better place to raise my children with all the nonsense in the world." Clay is president of Cash Family Investments, comprised of ranching and real estate and oil and gas investments, and president of the Don-Kay-Clay Cash Foundation.

The family's been very generous with Texas Tech. The Cash Family Sports Nutrition Center is the hub of the Athletics Department's nutrition program for 400-plus student-athletes. They funded the clubhouse and golf team facilities at the Rawls Course. They established an endowment, providing scholarships and support to various Texas Tech colleges and programs. And Clay is a member of the Texas Tech Foundation board, and his mom has served on some university search committees.

"We are here because this is where we got our start—the relationships—and we believe in giving back. Our foundation gives to a lot of things, but Tech is one of our favorites," said Clay, who likes how the foundation work models philanthropy for his kids.

When the Cashes lived in Salt Lake City, their next-door neighbor was Karl Malone—the "Mailman"—who played for the NBA's Utah Jazz and was named one of the seventy-five greatest NBA players of all time. Malone had some problems with people handling his money and asked Kay to help. Clay was 15 at the time and at the age where he was getting busier with his own life, so Kay dived in to help Malone. She became his gatekeeper and enforcer. Kay guided Malone through those years with a little help from Don. Even after they moved back to Lubbock, the Cashes stayed in touch with Malone.

And even when the family was away from the 806, Texas Tech was represented in their house and offices. The Cashes traveled to Texas Tech bowl games. Clay spent a number of his summers in West Texas. After Malone held a basketball camp in the Aloha State, Clay said he wanted to attend the University of Hawaii. But "my dad said, 'No way in hell,'" said Clay, and he was on his way to Lubbock.

Image courtesy of Texas Tech Communications and Marketing

Scott Dueser

Scott Dueser was Courtney Jordan's first call when raising money for the Excellence in Banking program at Texas Tech's Rawls College of Business. Jordan prodded her former boss at Abilene-based First Financial Bank about his previously stated interest in helping. Roughly a decade before, when Dueser and Jordan worked together, he mentioned how the bank got great employees from Texas A&M and San Houston State because they had banking programs.

"Texas Tech has got to do a banking program," he said of his alma mater. Years after Jordan approached him, Dueser placed some strategic calls to other bankers, not caring if they were competitors because the cause was good for West Texas banks and Texas Tech. In six months, $11 million was raised.

Dueser's been called Texas Tech's biggest fan. He graduated in 1975 with two degrees (in finance and accounting), chaired the Texas Tech University System Board of Regents, served on the Texas Tech Foundation Board and numerous other boards, and has given back financially.

It all started with an intervention—of sorts. Dueser grew up in Breckenridge, a bit more than 200 miles southeast of Lubbock. His plans after high school were to go a bit more than 200 miles in the other direction, to the University of Texas. Only two students from his high school class were going to Austin. Many others were going to Texas Tech, and several came by Dueser's house one summer night.

"They said, 'You're not going to Texas; you're going to Tech with us.' That's when the hippie movement was going on and Texas was not the place to be," Dueser said. So he changed course.

"One of the best decisions I've made in my life," he said. Dueser loved what he called Texas Tech's wholesome environment: good values and work ethic. He was a member of Beta Theta Pi and in the University Center leadership. That was in addition to taking eighteen units a semester to complete his two degrees in four years plus a summer session. "My degree is worth a lot more than when I graduated because Tech has continued to excel. I graduated from a mid-size university in West Texas. It's not that anymore," he said.

He's been generous—though he wasn't able to do so at first. When John Montford became the Texas Tech University System's first chancellor in the mid-1990s, he asked Dueser for a $100,000 donation at an Abilene event Dueser hosted for Montford. Dueser said he couldn't manage the gift then because he was looking at paying for college for four kids.

"I said, 'I'm gonna give you a lot more than that'—and I have. But it's because he asked me to give that inspired me to make sure I did," he said. Some of that came by becoming a conduit to help Texas Tech and Abilene grow together. Dueser helped raise the money for Texas Tech University Health Sciences Center to create a School of Nursing, the Jerry H. Hodge School of Pharmacy, and the Graduate School of Biomedical Sciences.

"Scott saw an opportunity for Abilene," said Jordan, adding that if the schools didn't end up in Abilene, students would have had to go elsewhere, which would have hurt the Abilene medical community. Jordan added, "It was just brilliant. It was a win-win-win for the community, the students, and Texas Tech. If you want something done, he's the one you go to—he's so unselfish with his time."

Images courtesy of the Dueser family

Dueser loved what he called Texas Tech's wholesome environment: good values and work ethic.

Robert Duncan

Chancellor Emeritus Robert Duncan was accustomed to hobnobbing with the power brokers in the state of Texas. He was used to shooting the breeze with tycoons and entrepreneurs, sports franchise owners and moguls, politicians and influencers. He had served in the Texas legislature for over two decades and had been a vital voice for fundamental improvements in the state. He was a champion of higher education, both in the Texas House of Representatives and the Texas State Senate, creating such programs as the National Research University Fund (NRUF) and the Texas Research Incentive Program (TRIP), even before he became the fourth chancellor of the Texas Tech University System. Deep down, Bob Duncan knew he owed so much of who he is and what he accomplished to the educational opportunities and privileges he experienced at Texas Tech.

And Chancellor Duncan has Texas Tech in his blood. Raised in West Texas, Duncan has two former regents in his family: Marshall Formby, his uncle, and Clint Formby, his cousin. So it was fated that he would attend Tech, receiving first his bachelor's degree in agricultural economics and serving as the student body president, and then his doctorate of jurisprudence from the TTU School of Law. And even while he enjoyed a successful law practice in Lubbock and built strong relationships with people on both sides of the aisle in Austin, he never forgot the faculty, staff, and students who had helped to make it all possible.

Perhaps that is why he was so committed to ensuring that Texas Tech and the Texas Tech University System would have the resources it needed to serve the community, the recognition it needed to expand its reach, the respect it earned to stand shoulder to shoulder with some of the best colleges and universities in the world. In his four-year tenure as chancellor (2014–2018), Duncan helped raise over $615 million in philanthropic funds. And he would talk with anyone who would listen about what Texas Tech was doing, where it was going, how it reached beyond the horizon.

That horizon would expand, under his leadership, to include the TTU Health Sciences Center El Paso Woody L. Hunt School of Dental Medicine and the TTU School of Veterinary Medicine (SVM). The SVM, founded in great measure due to Chancellor Duncan's commitment to West Texas and its rural communities, to Texas Tech, and to the great state of Texas, is the first of its kind to open in over 100 years. "Addressing the veterinary education needs in Texas is crucial not only because of the region's and state's deep-rooted history with agriculture and ranching but also because of its continued prosperity," Duncan has said of the SVM. "Our vision goes beyond the establishment of a veterinary school, setting out to transform the landscape of veterinary medicine education and provide innovative solutions for the industry's future." Fittingly, the beautiful open plaza at the SVM's south entrance is named after the advocate who helped to make it all happen.

As chancellor of the TTU System, Duncan never forgot why he wanted the job. He never forgot what made Texas Tech so special: the people. So at every awards ceremony, Chancellor Duncan was there. He congratulated the faculty who were recognized for their research and teaching excellence. He commended the staff members—the administrative assistants, the custodians, the hospitality and housing crew members, and so many others at the Staff Awards Ceremony—and thanked them for their tireless efforts to keep Texas Tech running, to make Texas Tech beautiful, to make Texas Tech inclusive, to make Texas Tech home.

Images courtesy of the Duncan family

As chancellor of the TTU System, Duncan never forgot why he wanted the job. He never forgot what made Texas Tech so special: the people.

Rick Francis

Rick Francis figures he was in Texas A&M gear in every photo taken of him the first few years of his life. His dad Larry was a proud Aggie—his nickname was "Ag." When it was time to go to college, the younger Francis told his father he wanted to go to the University of Texas with his friends. This was not well received. No son of Larry's was going to be a dang Tea Sip. Father and son fought over this topic most of the young man's senior year at El Paso's Coronado High School. So the latter drove to Lubbock, to check out different colors than maroon and burnt orange.

He'd never been on the Texas Tech campus but felt a bond, a sense of belonging, and enrolled. Ag—who served as El Paso's mayor—never got over his son's decision.

"He came to see me two times in four years," said Francis, an El Paso banker who long after graduation served three terms on the Texas Tech University System's Board of Regents. "And you can guess what those two times were—when A&M played football at Texas Tech."

Ag's Aggies won during his two visits, but Texas Tech turned out to be the right fit for the son of an Aggie. Francis matured during his four years as a Red Raider. He met the girl of his dreams, Ginger, and they've been married for more than four decades. He played intramural soccer.

As president of his SAE fraternity, he acquired leadership abilities that have propelled him through a successful career.

"They don't teach leadership skills at an academic university, and a fraternity is a testing ground for that. It helps you hone your skills because you've got to build consensus, have some strategic thinking, and, to the degree you're able—advance the fraternity on your watch. It gives you confidence going forward," he said.

He worked his way through college in the credit department at the downtown Sears department store—"the Amazon of its day," as Francis put it—moving with them to the new South Plains Mall when it opened. Francis got a degree in finance, then went to the Texas Tech School of Banking. He went on to a successful business career in El Paso and has been very involved in his hometown. Francis stayed in touch with his SAE frat brothers and still talks to some of them weekly. Then there's an annual get-together at a friend's ranch in Sweetwater.

His second act at Texas Tech started with the first of his three terms as a regent for the Texas Tech University System.

Ag's dream to be an A&M regent was never realized. But when his son became a regent, Francis felt that his dad was proud. Francis was chair of the Board of Regents during the 2005 legislative session and was walking the halls of the state capitol. "Legislators were saying, 'You're not a system; you're two schools across the street from each other and decided to call yourself a system,'" Francis said he was told.

Challenge accepted. Plans developed to grow the system faster than the legislature would fund it by partnering with West Texas communities. Amarillo stepped up to help fund a pharmacy school. Abilene underwrote the School of Public Health. El Paso raised hundreds of millions to create a four-year medical school. As the system grew across West Texas, Francis emphasized, its influence grew politically, and its health sciences presence was now bigger than Texas A&M's.

Images courtesy of the Texas Tech Board of Regents

Texas Tech turned out to be the right fit for the son of an Aggie.

Francis with his wife, Ginger

Kent Hance

People know a lot about Kent Hance because the Chancellor Emeritus's powerful personality, quips, and stories, accompanied by his textbook West Texas accent, are hard to overlook.

But not every story is known. Kent Hance once got a call from Jim Rock, one of Hance's staff aides when he represented West Texas in the US Congress. Rock helped his boss immensely in writing the 1981 Hance-authored tax bill for President Ronald Reagan. Rock knew a girl from Arlington, Virginia—No. 1 in her high school class. She was a "dreamer" whose parents entered the country without documents but with hopes for a better life for their daughter. The girl was having a hard time getting into college.

So Hance, decades after he left Congress and now Texas Tech University System chancellor, flew the girl down to Lubbock. She liked the school, and Hance was able to line up some scholarship money for her at his alma mater. She graduated. Before she left Lubbock for medical school, Hance hosted a dinner at the Texas Tech Club for the young woman and her parents and friends.

"I feel blessed. I've been able to make quite a bit of money and I've always tried to give back, help people. I get a blessing out it," said Hance.

When it comes to Texas Tech, the man whose mother told him he'd never be a little fish has been loud, proud, and accomplished. Hance and his mom were in their car after visiting the principal of Dimmitt High School to discuss where he could go to college. "He said, 'Kent needs to decide if he wants to be a big fish in a little pond like West Texas A&M or a little fish in a big pond at Tech,'" Hance recalled. After that conversion, Hance's mother got very serious and told her son: "Don't you *ever, ever* let somebody tell you that you're going to be a small fish."

Hance went to Tech, majored in finance, pledged Delta Tau Delta, and became a Saddle Tramp. One of his fraternity brothers was Ed Whitacre, and one of his fellow Saddle Tramps was Jerry Rawls—both are featured in this book for their accomplishments and for sharing their success with their alma mater. Hance went to law school in Austin and came back to teach at Tech, while starting his law practice and keeping his eye on opportunities in politics.

Hance took office as Texas Tech's third chancellor in late 2006—or, as Red Raider receiver Michael Crabtree called him, "the Hancellor." He set ambitious goals—by 2020: 40,000 Tech students, 5,000 TTUHSC students, and 10,000 Angelo State University students. Those goals were reached. A billion-dollar fundraising campaign goal did even better than hoped, raising $1.2 billion. In addition, Tech moved toward Carnegie R1 status with "very high research activity" and got there two years after he left office. He donated money for a chapel named for him on the southeast corner of campus.

The Saddle Tramp always felt his main job was to be Texas Tech's biggest cheerleader. He understood how the university, Lubbock, and West Texas felt in the shadow of other, older institutions for decades. Hance believed that the time for that kind of thinking was over. "At graduations I'd say, 'Dream no little dreams if you're a Texas Tech graduate. If you're going to dream little dreams, go to Texas or A&M.'"

Image courtesy of the Southwest Collection / Special Collections Library

Bob L. Herd

Before a 2008 ceremony announcing Bob Herd's $15 million gift to Texas Tech's Petroleum Engineering Department, Kent Hance asked Herd to say a few words. "No, I'm not a lawyer. I'm an oil man. I'm not a talker," Herd told Chancellor Hance. But Herd's wife Pat got her husband to agree to the request. After a few people made comments, Herd got up. "Bob put a death grip on the podium," Hance recalled. "I thought he was going to squeeze the wood out of the podium. And he looked at the audience for 15 seconds." It was a long enough pause to make folks anxious. "And then he gave the best speech ever given at Tech. He said, 'Thank you, Texas Tech. You gave me the key.' His voice quivered and he sat down."

Herd may not have enjoyed public speaking, but he was a dynamic businessman who shared his massive success with his alma mater and others before he passed away in 2019.

He almost attended university elsewhere. It was only after missing the deadline to apply to the University of Texas that someone suggested he go two hours north to Texas Tech. He started in the spring semester on the GI Bill, studying petroleum engineering. Herd graduated in 1957 at a time when oil prices dropped to under one dollar and there were few jobs. Being a little older and having a military background helped him get a job. The company gave him a field to manage, and he learned the business. Herd Production started in 1965. The first eight of nine wells were successful and eventually he had hundreds of wells in Texas and Louisiana. Herd's grandson Michael—a 2010 Texas Tech graduate—now runs the company and the Bob L. Herd Foundation, which has been generous to Tech and Tyler, where the company is based.

"We love Texas Tech. We like to say it's not SMU, in the middle of Highland Park. It's not UT in the middle of Austin. You have to want to come to Texas Tech. That takes a special type of student, a special type of person. That's why Red Raiders are so successful and so well received," said Michael in a 2021 interview.

Michael Herd said his family have been active over the years promoting Texas Tech. Michael did team and calf roping at Texas Tech and had a Professional Rodeo Cowboys Association card. He's married to Whitney Wolfe Herd, the billionaire entrepreneur who developed Bumble, an online dating site that empowers women, a mission that even an old oilman cared to support. "Empowering women, equality, financial independence for women—those are all things my grandfather and I believed in," said Michael, who said his grandfather advised his then-girlfriend as she was developing Bumble. Bob Herd was also best man at Michael and Whitney's wedding.

Herd may not have been comfortable speaking to crowds he didn't know but, as his grandson related, he had no problem getting his point across running his company. "He was a humble man who was proud of what he had. But he didn't need the judgment of others. It was about giving back to something that gave so much to him," he said.

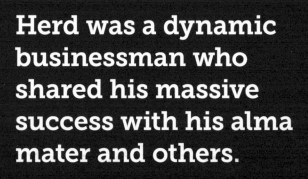

Herd was a dynamic businessman who shared his massive success with his alma mater and others.

Arch Lamb

Archibald "Arch" Green Lamb served as a zealous promoter of Texas Tech University and became one of Lubbock County's most respected citizens. He was born in Coolidge, Texas, in 1912, but moved to Lubbock with only seventy-five dollars in his pocket to attend Texas Technological College in 1935. He worked at the campus creamery for twenty-five cents per hour. He famously shined shoes, leading to his election as "Yell Leader." He served on the student council and as vice-president of the student body. Notably, Arch founded the iconic Saddle Tramps, channeling the previously disruptive enthusiasm of rowdy students to create what is today a revered Tech spirit organization. Around the same time, by dressing in a so-called "Zorro outfit" to maintain anonymity, classmate Gene Tate and Arch "borrowed" a palomino stallion from the Ag Pavilion and rode around the football field during 1936 home games at halftime. The exploits perhaps inspired, years later, Joe Kirk Fulton's emergence at the 1954 Gator Bowl as the first official Masked Rider. Lamb and the Saddle Tramps influenced the Victory Bells and Carol of Lights traditions as well. Arch graduated in 1939 with a bachelor's degree in dairy manufacturing.

After college, Arch worked for creameries elsewhere in Texas, eventually resettling in Lubbock and becoming the county commissioner for Precinct 1, a post he held from January 1955 to December 1976. Contemporaries respected Arch as a diligent and frugal public servant. He supported divided highways and the creation of Loop 289. He served the West Texas Museum, the Ranching Heritage Center, the First Methodist Church, the Rotary Club of Lubbock, and the Masons. His business, Lamb's Milk and Ice Cream, was innovative. He raised crops on his farm situated on land where, now, the West End Center shopping development is located. He also had a penchant for raising mules.

Arch campaigned against demolition of the Texas Tech Dairy Barn. He proselytized about how many first-generation Tech scholars put themselves through college with the earnings from the sale of milk from student- or college-owned dairy cows. In the 1990s, he helped raise over $64,000 to refurbish the edifice, which Tech administrators ultimately restored into an event center and offices for the College of Agricultural Sciences and Natural Resources.

Arch met Mina Marie Wolf of Sagerton, Texas, and the couple married in 1941. Mina received her BA in chemistry and MS in food and nutrition during the 1930s from Tech, then a PhD in nutrition from Columbia University in 1941. She returned to Tech as assistant professor of food and nutrition and served as department chair and as the first Margaret W. Weeks Professor of Home Economics, retiring in 1975. Arch was inducted into the Tech Athletic Hall of Fame; became a Distinguish Alumnus; and the Goin' Band and Saddle Tramps sections of the east bleachers at Jones AT&T Stadium were named in honor of Arch and Mina. At his death in 2004, Will Rogers and Soapsuds were wrapped in black crepe as a final tribute to Arch Lamb—the first Saddle Tramp.

Image courtesy of the Southwest Collection / Special Collections Library

Arch founded the iconic Saddle Tramps to create what is today a revered Tech spirit organization.

Pete and Nelda Laney

Pete Laney saw a couple walk past him before a Texas Tech basketball game in the early 1960s. He knew the guy and knew *of* the girl through mutual friends. Laney was with a buddy. They had an empty seat next to them in the Lubbock Municipal Coliseum—back when it was a shiny new showplace.

"I've got one seat for your girlfriend, but none for you," Laney said to tease the guy, who didn't take it well and stalked off to catch up with his date. The girl caught Laney's eye, and his friend bet him $10 he couldn't get a date with her. So he called the young woman, Nelda McQuien, a few days later and she agreed to go out with him. Before they graduated from Texas Tech, Pete and Nelda wed, and they were married for 53 years before Nelda died in 2016.

Over the years, Pete and Nelda became a powerful pair for West Texas and their alma mater. Pete ignored his farmer father's wishes and became a farmer, before getting into politics and eventually becoming Speaker of the Texas House of Representatives for a decade. Nelda—besides being First Lady of the House, which she helped restore to its original design—had a massive impact on the Texas Tech Alumni Association. She led the fundraising drive for the McKenzie-Merket Alumni Center expansion project and was president of the Alumni Association's National Board of Directors. Nelda also started the Official Texas Tech Ornament program to raise scholarship money, patterning it after a similar Texas Legislature ornament program.

When Pete was Speaker of the House, he put a then-record number of women representatives in leadership positions. The move ticked off some of the older men in the legislature who'd been around for a while and felt they were owed those posts, but they were not Pete's role models.

"My wife taught me how much more dependable women are than men in terms of making things happen," he said. She also held her own with her Speaker/husband. They were talking about how their Texas Tech diplomas were exactly alike—but Nelda pointed out one small difference. "Hers said 'with honors,'" said Pete, smiling in the kitchen of his Lubbock home.

Besides getting a degree in agriculture economics, Pete stated, one of the most valuable things he learned at Texas Tech was meeting people from all over Texas. Not everyone was like the folks in his hometown of Hale Center or Nelda's hometown of Plainview. He learned how to make things happen in his fraternity. This helped him guide the legislative process during his years in Austin. "I didn't care if a bill was brought by a Republican or Democrat as long as it was good government," said the lifelong Democrat who respected people's differences. He had a good relationship with Governor, and later President, George W. Bush.

And he was happy to help Texas Tech when he could. When the University of Texas chancellor came into Laney's office in the 1990s and said the Longhorns were fixing to leave the Southwest Conference, Laney asked if they'd take Tech with them. He did not get an affirmative answer. So Laney called Lieutenant Governor Bob Bullock—also a Red Raider—and gave him a heads-up. Bullock got things rolling, and by the time UT left to form the Big 12, Tech and Baylor were along for the ride.

Image courtesy of the Texas Tech Alumni Association

When Pete was Speaker of the House, he put a then-record number of women representatives in leadership positions.

Mark Lanier

Mark Lanier is a storyteller. He tells stories in a courtroom and from a pulpit, merging the two careers he pondered growing up in Lubbock. Almost twenty-five years after his graduating from the Texas Tech University School of Law, the Mark & Becky Lanier Professional Development Center opened in 2008—a huge addition to the law school. It housed—among other things—the Donald Hunt Courtroom. "Don Hunt changed my life and made me understand both the art and science of advocacy," Lanier said of his teacher. He learned well.

The Lanier Law Firm in Houston has offices in Oklahoma City, New York, and Los Angeles. He's built a reputation as one of the best trial lawyers in the country and has won massive judgments, particularly in cases against the pharmaceutical company Merck, for their drug Vioxx. "You've got to punish them. You can choose to speak as loud as you want. If you speak loudly enough, it registers. You can make the whole pharmaceutical industry hear," he told a jury in one such case. Lanier's been named the Trial Lawyer of the Year by the National Trial Lawyers, among a long list of honors and awards.

He's back often in his native Lubbock for events and to teach at his alma mater—or for a quick bite. "I can't tell you how many times I've flown from L.A. to Houston and put the plane down in Lubbock to get dinner at Taco Villa," he said. His obsession with Taco Villa rivals his love for Texas Tech. When two of his daughters decided—against his encouragement—to go to Baylor, those folks in Waco saw the successful attorney as a potential donor when he bought football tickets. They set up an account for Lanier and, to make it clear to them the limit of his support, he named it Raider Bear. "With Raider first," he emphasized. "We bleed Red and Black."

His wife, he jokes, has three degrees from Texas Tech. In addition to her bachelor's in international trade and master's in Spanish, Becky Lanier went to Tech Kindergarten. "She was finger painting a Double T before she could write her name," said her husband. Lanier studied Hebrew and Greek at Texas Tech in anticipation of preaching, but the university didn't offer a degree in biblical languages, and he transferred to David Lipscomb University in Nashville. Lanier keeps a foot in the pulpit teaching his Sunday school class. He's also written a number of Christian books and one law book.

He's always ready to help his hometown university and alma mater. "Texas Tech has one foot in the past and one foot in the future. Texas Tech has trained and taught and enabled people like me to find success in the world. The foot in the future is those students who are there now, getting prepared for their careers and to make their mark in the world. And there are more to follow. We always answer the call when needed," he said.

Images courtesy of the Texas Tech Alumni Association

Mark Lanier and teammates at Moot Court

Jack Maddox

Jack Maddox came from humble beginnings. He grew up in a family with nine children and was raised on a leased goat ranch in Menard, Texas. For Jack, 1929 was the year of endings and beginnings. His father died the year that marked the beginning of what we now know as the Great Depression, and the family was impoverished. Jack graduated from Texas Tech that year and became the great hope of the family.

Jack had entered Texas Tech as one of the very first students at the university in 1925 and graduated in 1929 with a degree in textile engineering. Upon his graduation, Jack was hired by Goodyear Tire Company in Akron, Ohio. The company was hiring textile engineers due to their familiarity with the materials and methods used to produce tires, and Jack was exhilarated to put his expertise to use. But Jack was one of those laid off on account of the devastating economic crash.

But Jack had a family to take care of. Unemployed and desperate for help, he turned to his former engineering professor and the first president of Texas Tech, Paul Whitfield Horn, and asked for mentorship and guidance. And Horn never turned his back on a student, especially not one willing to roll up his sleeves and work, and whom he had gotten to know so well because Jack had represented TTU as student body president. While we may never know what strings President Horn may have pulled, Jack interviewed with Texas Power and Light in Dallas. He was hired as a junior engineer and was transferred to Hobbs, New Mexico, in 1931.

Jack and his wife, Mabel, created in Hobbs a life of purpose and philanthropy. Jack cultivated a career in the utility industry and, driven by intellectual curiosity, pursued opportunities in real estate development, gas pipeline operations, and banking. The couple became leaders of the community and were especially dedicated to youth programs and higher education. Jack recognized that his success was rooted in people who had believed in him, in opportunities afforded him because of the university, in relationships that were built, developed, earned through trust, confidence, and loyalty. The two founded the J.F Maddox Foundation in 1963 to support the communities of southeastern New Mexico through student scholarships and foundation grants to nonprofit organizations and governmental entities.

Jack never forgot his family at Texas Tech. The J.F Maddox Foundation has generously supported the university by endowing several chairs in the Whitacre College of Engineering and through projects like the Maddox Engineering Research Center, a cutting-edge facility that sustains the innovative endeavors of faculty, staff, and students. Housing the labs and studios for the National Academy of Engineering faculty, the center allows the Whitacre College to continue its foundational work of engaging with the grand challenges we face as a community of global scholars.

Jack did not have any children, so the children of Jack's brother, Donovan, carry on the work of their uncle and their father. As Jim, the president of the J.F Maddox Foundation, explained at the opening of the center, "These two brothers [Jack and Donovan Maddox] took full advantage of the education they received at Texas Tech. . . . It is our hope that the Maddox Engineering Research Center will enable current and future Texas Tech students to have available even greater opportunities as a result of their matriculation at this outstanding university."

Top right: From left to right: Mabel Maddox, Jack Maddox, Donovan Maddox.
Images courtesy of the J.F Maddox Foundation

Jack recognized that his success was rooted in people who had believed in him, in opportunities afforded him because of the university, in relationships that were built, developed, earned through trust, confidence, and loyalty.

Tibor Nagy

Tibor Nagy fled Hungary in 1956 with his parents, after the Hungarian Revolution failed, because his father faced execution. They got to Vienna and were there a few months. The CIA wanted to bring Nagy's dad to America and use the former Hungarian Army colonel as an asset. Part of that process meant visiting the American Embassy in Vienna. As a little communist growing up in Hungary, Nagy was told Americans were evil, despicable, ugly, and mean. "I did not want to go to the American Embassy and see all these nasty people who might eat or kill me," he later said. The people were kind, however, and they changed his mind. If he got to America, he decided, he wanted to be an American diplomat.

The Nagy family came to the US in 1957, spending time in a refugee camp in New Jersey. The family settled in Washington, DC. By the time Nagy was ready for college, he wanted to be an architect; his dad was a civil engineer. Cost was an issue, and Texas Tech got on Nagy's radar—he who'd never been west of Pennsylvania.

As he came into town from the airport, Lubbock seemed to him like one big suburb. But he quickly became fond of the city and Texas Tech. His roommate was from Abernathy. The roommate's family adopted him—after making sure he wasn't a Communist. He did not do well in the architecture program his first year so instead revisited his dream of becoming a diplomat. He also met a young woman named Jane who grew up on a farm between Plainview and Lockney. They got married before he graduated. After graduation, the Nagys drove to Washington in a Mustang. Jane finished her education and Nagy passed the Foreign Service exam.

When it came time for Nagy's first post, he was given a list of twenty-one places in the world, among them Ouagadougou, Bamako, Djibouti, Niamey—and Lusaka, the capital of Zambia. The Nagys had heard nice things from the Zambian ambassador, so they picked Lusaka and loved Africa and warmth of the African people. Within a year of being in Zambia, they had triplets. They had eight postings over the years, with the highlights being ambassador to Guinea and Ethiopia during the Clinton and George W. Bush administrations. When it was time for his overseas service to end, Nagy became ambassador-in-residence at the University of Oklahoma. When Idris Traylor retired as executive director of Tech's Office of International Affairs, he contacted Nagy to see if he'd be interested in replacing him.

Thanks to Nagy's influence, Texas Tech sent more and more students to its centers in Spain and Costa Rica. The university dramatically increased the number of students coming to Texas Tech from other countries. But Nagy wasn't done with the State Department, eventually running the embassy in Nigeria and becoming Assistant Secretary of State for African Affairs—the highest State Department post a Red Raider has held.

While working in Africa, Nagy wanted to flip the narrative. "Africa had always been seen as a problem to be solved, not an opportunity. We should look at Africa through the windshield, not the rearview mirror. Africa is all about the young people and developing the private sector," he said. Again, it was something he had picked up in West Texas.

"Lubbock represents the real essence of the American spirit. There's an openness here to creative thinking. There is a sense and appreciation of hard work, entrepreneurship. It's the kind of environment for starting a business. The people are blessed with what I call eminent common sense," he said.

Image courtesy of Texas Tech Communications and Marketing

W. B. Rushing

On the day in 1923 that the cornerstone was laid for Texas Technological College's Administration Building, W. B. "Dub" Rushing was there as a member of the Plainview High School band.

Four years later, Rushing arrived as an architecture student and became a Distinguished Alum—the only one not to have finished a degree. Rushing left a massive impact on Texas Tech and Lubbock in a decades-long career as a successful businessman, playing a key role in developing Lubbock over its first half-century. Rushing was also a philanthropist, sharing his success with Tech, giving millions toward scholarships and other areas.

He sold a burger stand to open the Varsity Bookstore in 1934—an iconic business that spurred more development around campus. Rushing founded Briercroft Savings & Loan. He and his brother built Lubbock's first shopping center on 19th Street and Avenue N. "He was a visionary," Rushing's friend Henry Huneke told the *Lubbock Avalanche-Journal* when 97-year-old Rushing died in 2007. "This city wouldn't be what it is today without the Dub Rushings. He's not the only one, but in his time, he was the one." Rushing was very active in Lubbock and played tennis into his 90s. He also coached the game, and a Lubbock city tennis center is named for him. But what comes up over and over when people discuss Rushing is the word shrewd—especially when it came to evaluating and buying land. Rushing had a knack for both doing deals and providing Red Raiders with valuable business experience.

Many years ago, a certain Texas Tech graduate was back in Lubbock teaching at his alma mater. He'd heard Rushing was the best businessman in town and asked him if he could learn from him. The man went with Rushing to Childress, where he had a mobile home manufacturing plant. Rushing was meeting a potential buyer, who was flying in from Houston on his own plane. But they could not strike a deal. On the drive back to Lubbock, Rushing told his young friend, "You gotta keep fishing. Don't get discouraged on not completing a deal so that you start doing bad deals."

A few weeks later, Rushing asked the younger man to come with him to Wichita Falls. Rushing was looking for land to build a grocery store for Furr's and drugstore for Raff and Hall. They found land with a sign so weathered it was hard to make out the phone number. Rushing told his young charge to call the number and find out how much the owner wanted. Then Rushing added if his new colleague could get an offer for less than $100,000, he'd give him $10,000. But *do not* give the owner a number, he added. Rushing's "student" was making $9,500 teaching at Tech at the time—so this would double his annual earnings.

The landowner claimed he had a lot of takers, which didn't seem right given how old the sign looked. The owner wouldn't give a price and the young man said he'd hang up. That's when the owner said, "OK—$25,000!" The young man was stunned and yelled into the phone: "$25,000!" He hadn't intended the outburst to be a bargaining tool; it was said out of surprise. But then the owner said, "OK—$15,000!"

Decades later, a reception was held for Kent Hance, newly appointed chancellor for the Texas Tech University System. Rushing attended. When he and Hance shook hands, Rushing said, "25,000!" recalling their successful day in Wichita Falls.

Linda Rutherford

Linda Rutherford wanted to be a newspaper reporter from the time she was 12 years old, sparked by the TV show *Lou Grant*. Grant was played by Ed Asner, extending the role he made famous from the *Mary Tyler Moore Show*—a gruff boss with high standards. The show inspired people toward a journalism career.

When it was time to pick a college, Rutherford considered the trio of Texas Tech, the University of Texas, and Trinity University in San Antonio. Trinity's Mother Superior looked over the student newspaper every night before it went to press. Deal breaker. Burnt Orange journalism students were limited to one semester on the school paper to make room for others. Deal breaker. At Texas Tech, Rutherford could start at the then-named *University Daily* as a freshman writing briefs and could advance. Welcome to Lubbock.

She was editor her senior year. Rutherford's *University Daily* covered serious issues like hazing in the Greek system, police response rates, emergency phone stations that were not working, and early attempts by a then-called LGBT group to be officially recognized. Rutherford ended up at the *Dallas Times Herald* after a few other stops following graduation and covered the airline industry. In 1992, her newspaper was bought by the rival *Dallas Morning News*, which announced plans to shut down the *Times Herald*. She made a safe landing in a Southwest Airlines public relations job. It was as good a fit as Texas Tech had been. Three decades later she's executive vice president, people & communications and chief communications officer—one of the airline's five executive vice presidents. "I never for a moment thought from my time at Texas Tech I'd be sitting here as an executive vice president of Southwest Airlines, but it's a tribute to Texas Tech," she said.

Rutherford was raised in a single-parent home in Carrollton and learned that if she wanted something, she had to make it happen. Throw in a chip-on-the-shoulder attitude she shared with many other Red Raiders because the school on the dusty South Plains was not seen as an equal to older Texas universities. "We knew we were the underdog. We had to show what we were made of to be able to shine on the same stage," she said. She learned a strong work ethic and the importance of teamwork and believing in yourself. She praised faculty and staff for providing a great learning environment.

Running the student paper was like running a business: leading people, meeting deadlines, getting everything right, working with the advertising staff to make sure there was enough money coming through the door. At Southwest, she worked with the airline's late founder, the irreverent Herb Kelleher. She admired his incredible vocabulary and shared a love of words.

Now she's responsible for human resources, employee learning and development, communications and community outreach, diversity/equity/inclusion, and a group called culture and engagement. She's grateful for the university that set her on a successful path. "Because my parents were divorced, I knew college was going to be really tough. There was no savings plan to pay for it. I scratched for every scholarship I could find," she said.

Her degree opened doors and her experience gave her the confidence to walk through those doors.

She's given back by establishing an endowed scholarship in the College of Media & Communication, served on that college's national advisory board, chaired the Texas Tech Alumni Association National Board of Directors, and was on the search committee that picked Lawrence Schovanec as Texas Tech's seventeenth president.

Images courtesy of Southwest Airlines

"I never for a moment thought from my time at Texas Tech I'd be sitting here as an executive vice president of Southwest Airlines, but it's a tribute to Texas Tech."

Jim Sowell

The name Jim Sowell is legendary on Texas Tech campus, not because his character is Texas large or because he boasts of his generosity but because he helped to shape this campus in some of the most powerful ways, always with graciousness, humility, and kindness.

Born in Bryan, Texas, Sowell graduated from Texas Tech in 1970 with a degree in finance. The big West Texas skies inspired him to think broadly not only about his business ventures but also about his cultural impact at Texas Tech. After serving two years in the US Army, Sowell began building his construction empire, founding Jim Sowell Construction, Co., Inc. in 1972, one of the largest subdivision developers in the State of Texas. He also was a majority stockholder in American General Hospitality, Inc., the largest operator of Hilton Hotels in the world. He served on the board of directors of several New York Stock Exchange companies, including NL Industries, Todd Shipyards Corporation, and Ketchum Drug Company, the Board of Directors for the Governor's Business Council, the Dallas Citizens Council, the Central Dallas Ministries, the Dallas Museum of Art, and Baylor Hospital, and held the position of President of the Boy Scouts of America.

Sowell never forgot the school that gave him his foundation, and he gave his time, wisdom, and expertise as chair of the Board of Regents of the Texas Tech University System. And he comes back to his alma mater to inspire his fellow Red Raiders. He encourages TTU students to think about their investment in their own education.

Sowell did not originally plan on attending Texas Tech. Even as a young child, going to high school and waking up at the crack of dawn to deliver newspapers, the plan was to go to A&M. His father had gone there, and he expected he would follow in his father's footsteps. But during the Vietnam War, being a member of ROTC was a mandatory requirement at A&M and he was not certain he wanted to go to a school that guaranteed he would go to war. And since his dad, a loyal Aggie, also promised Sowell $100 a month if he attended ANY state school other than the University of Texas at Austin, he set his sights on Texas Tech.

He has never not had Texas Tech in his vision and in his heart. Whether it be supporting his fellow Texas Tech alumni in drilling for clean water in Kenya or endowing one of the very first sports position scholarships for Texas Tech Athletics, Sowell has demonstrated his love of all things Texas Tech. One such example is the creation of the James Sowell Family Collection in Literature, Community and the Natural World housed in the Texas Tech University Southwest Collection and Special Collections Library. The expansiveness of the Sowell Family Collection includes drafts of novels, letters, memoirs, diaries, photographs, sketches, memos, and other artifacts of writers who deal extensively with the natural world, from plants to animals, Arctic to desert, flood to wildfire. A group of faculty members, led by Honors College professor Kurt Caswell, inspired by E. O. Wilson's book *Consilience* and bolstered by support from Sowell, chair of the Board of Regents at the time, sought out the papers of a group of writers who could bring together, in literary, historical, scholarly fashion, the areas of science and the humanities in the natural realm, anchored by the works of National Book Award winner, Barry Lopez.

Image courtesy of the Southwest Collection / Special Collections Library

Dale Swinburn

A fertilizer salesman visited Dale Swinburn's Tulia farm and tried to sell him a line of bull.

The salesman didn't know how to test Dale's soil to determine exactly what was necessary to enhance the West Texas farmland. But Dale learned how to test soil and a lot more at Texas Tech. What he learned prepared him to be a successful farmer and businessman and to know what he needed from a pile of manure.

Dale is one of thousands of graduates from what is now known as the Davis College of Agricultural Sciences and Natural Resources, what was originally known as CASNR and before that the School of Agriculture, one of the original four schools when classes at Texas Technological College first began.

Dale went to Texas Tech because his mother—who back then made $5,000 a year as a teacher—had attended Southern Methodist University in Dallas and saw her parents almost starve to afford private higher education for her and her sister. Dale showed up in 1960 to study history and, like his parents, be a teacher. But he decided to farm and changed majors. Dale needed five years to graduate, but his father told him, "We all have a right to change our mind. You should do what you want to do." Years later, he's still impressed with the curriculum that challenged him. "They were ingenious," he said, adding he's used all of it over his career.

While he was in Lubbock, Dale started dating Cheryl, his future wife. The couple grew up in Tulia. Dale won Cheryl's heart because he was willing to drive to her house about twenty miles outside of town; other boys wanted to meet her in town.

After graduating from Tech, Dale started farming on a small amount of land his parents had. Land was important to his folks. "My mom always said, 'Save your money and buy land,'" he said. The Swinburns spent decades growing cotton and grain and raising some livestock in Tulia. Then Dale and four others opened a successful cotton gin business in 1978. Including Dale, three of the five were Red Raiders.

Dale's also been very involved with his alma mater. He's served on the Texas Tech Foundation Board of Directors—brought on by his old friend Kent Hance, then chancellor of the Texas Tech University System. They attended Texas Tech together, and Dale remembers Hance teasing him about whose high school was better—Hance's Dimmitt Bobcats or Dale's Tulia Hornets.

Dale also served on CASNR advisory committees. He and Cheryl have donated to the Dairy Barn renovation and other facilities. When he looks back to 1960 when he arrived on campus, Dale said the biggest change is the number of women in CASNR compared to the minuscule number back then. What hasn't changed? "Good people," he said. "I can get teary-eyed about Texas Tech. It's been a very important part of our lives."

Part of that appeal is Texas Tech football. The Swinburns have had season tickets for years. Cheryl didn't go to Texas Tech—she had a basketball scholarship to Wayland Baptist to be a Flying Queen—but has become a Red Raider by osmosis. "A lot of our friends are Red Raiders," she said. Two of their three sons live in Lubbock. All three sons are Red Raiders and one grandson in middle school has already told his grandparents he'll go to Texas Tech. And there's one more Texas Tech connection. Their oldest grandson's other grandfather was the late Red Raider legend E. J. Holub, a member of the Ring of Honor and a Super Bowl winner.

Photo by Artie Limmer

J. T. and Margaret Talkington

When J. T. and Margaret Talkington came to Lubbock in 1946, they did not know that they would be changing the landscape of the city forever. Their generosity, vision, and reach are virtually unmatched—as is their love for the community, the arts, and the possibilities this little West Texas town and Texas Tech University could open up for its people.

J. T. and Margaret married in 1939, and after J. T. served in the US Navy during the Second World War, he joined Patterson, Leatherwood, and Miller, a CPA firm that was moving into West Texas. Margaret thought she could bring style to the South Plains, founding Margaret's Ladies Specialty Store which would provide fashion, confidence, and a sense of self to women in Lubbock. She traveled by train from Lubbock to New York City to meet people, sign an agreement with buyers, and set up a line of credit for her new business. So influential did Margaret become that the store became known as the "Neimans of West Texas," and many wanted to be known as a "Margaret's woman." But her eye for style extended beyond silks and taffetas into aesthetics and art. Margaret was a dear friend of sculptor Glenna Goodacre, and her collection featured several of Goodacre's pieces as well as other works by well-known local, state, national, and international artists.

For decades, even as they built their businesses, the couple built a community. Through finance, fashion, and art, J. T. and Margaret Talkington changed the shape, look, and culture of Lubbock. Their commitment to Lubbock and the local community was honored in the establishment of the J. T. and Margaret Talkington Charitable Foundation in 1997, and through its good works and generosity, it has provided funding for "arts and culture, community-based education, youth services, and other areas of community improvement."

That umbrella also covered Texas Tech University.

Not only have their undergraduate scholarships and graduate fellowships helped over 300 students a year, but their generosity helps to support the first comprehensive student-athlete leadership program of its kind in the United States. In an interview, Coach Marsha Sharp remembered that J. T. and Margaret didn't just provide philanthropic support—they were present and proud Texas Tech fans. "J. T. and Margaret were fans of both basketball programs at Texas Tech. They and about ten couples had a longstanding tradition of getting a trolley from someone's house to come to games—particularly when we were in the old [Lubbock Municipal] Coliseum—then go back to the house and have refreshments." The Talkingtons would come early to the games and wave to the players from the stands.

From athletics to arts, J. T. and Margaret Talkington saw beauty in all the facets of Texas Tech and the Lubbock community. No wonder then that the College of Visual & Performing Arts is named for these two patrons, who gave the largest gift in the history of the college to support the arts, music, dance, and theater in ways innumerable. Former chancellor Robert Duncan described their impact in this way: "The Talkingtons are remembered as truly unselfish, gracious people. They had a deep love for Lubbock and gave boundlessly to create a stronger community. Their generosity was indiscriminate, and we are so grateful they believed in and supported our vision for higher education in West Texas that impacts the world."

In 2010, Margaret Talkington, after her husband's death, was honored with the Heroes for Children Award by the Texas Education Agency. The Talkingtons did not have children of their own, but in one way or another they have touched all our lives.

Image courtesy of the Southwest Collection / Special Collections Library

Through finance, fashion, and art, J. T. and Margaret Talkington changed the shape, look, and culture of Lubbock.

FIGHTING FOR

TEXAS TECH

Sharon Moultrie Bruner

The youngest of five children, Sharon Moultrie was born in Pampa, Texas, on January 28, 1960. She tried out as a walk-on athlete in 1979 with the encouragement of Falecia Freeman, a sophomore lead performer on the Texas Tech's women's track and field team, and quickly captured the attention of Coach Beta Little. It was surprising that the first-year student had been overlooked by college recruiters given her high school track experience. Moultrie, who began competing in high school track and field competitions her junior year, displayed an obvious aptitude for the sport. By her senior year, she set the District 3A long-jump record of 18 feet 2.5 inches and placed third in regionals two weeks later. Coach Little recognized Moultrie's enormous potential in speed and distance jumping and immediately added her to the team.

Additionally, a friendly rivalry of sorts developed between Freeman and Moultrie that pushed both to perform better in individual events and as a group in team competitions. In fact, Moultrie found the team aspect to be the best part of the sport and cited the four-member 440 relay as her favorite event. Moultrie, Freeman, Pam Montgomery, and Tonya Jones formed a powerhouse of a sprint relay team for the Red Raiders.

During her first year at Texas Tech, Moultrie earned a full athletic scholarship and, over the course of the next three years, distinguished herself as a standout student and athlete. Described by Coach Little as "the kind of athlete every coach dreams about," Moultrie held fast to her mother's words of wisdom: "If you're going to do something, don't half-step it: do your best." Coach Jarvis Scott, the first American woman to qualify for both the 400- and 800-meter races in the Olympics, also played a big influence.

In 1981, Moultrie became the first African American as well as the first female athlete to be elected Homecoming Queen. She was also the first Texas Tech female athlete to earn All-American honors, for long jump in 1981 and 1982, and was a seven-time NCAA qualifier in sprint and jumping events. In April 1982, she won the Outstanding Senior Athlete Award, one of the university's top women's athletic prizes. After graduating in spring 1983 with a BS degree in physical education, Moultrie taught and coached boys' and girls' cross-country and girls' track at South Grand Prairie High School, where she was named Coach of the Year and Teacher of the Year. She married Raymond Edward Bruner and had two sons, Jarard Trent and Julian Treavor.

After more than thirty-six years in the profession, Coach Moultrie Bruner's many contributions to the sport continue to be acknowledged. In 1998, she was inducted into Texas Tech's Athletic Hall of Honor. In 2001, she was admitted into the Texas Black Sports Hall of Fame. In 2021, she was an inductee of the Texas Panhandle Sports Hall of Fame.

Images courtesy of the Southwest Collection / Special Collections Library
Bottom: Moultrie and Pam Montgomery

Peter Willis Cawthon

Peter Cawthon was born on March 24, 1898, in Houston, and came to the notion of coaching football at a young age. He was a great athlete at Central High and entered Southwestern University in 1917, earning multiple athletic letters and becoming known for his strict athletic and personal regimen. In 1919, he took his first coaching job at Beaumont High. He lied about his age, stating that he was 23, not 21, in order to appear not to be just slightly older than his charges.

In 1920, Cawthon directed freshmen sports at Rice Institute. The following year, he went to Terrill School for Boys. Success there took him to Austin College, which hired him as head coach in 1923. Ironically, Cawthon led his team against Texas Tech in Lubbock during its inaugural season, a game that ended in a 3–3 tie.

Tech's football team cratered in 1929, finishing 1–7–2 and embarrassing the school with rowdy behavior. President Horn sought a change and hired Cawthon. The latter instituted a rigorous regimen, and the team had a winning season in 1931, its last as an independent. Cawthon then arranged games against larger institutions and played a few against Border Conference teams. Success followed, with a mark of 25–5–1 between 1932 and 1934. The final year in this stretch featured the purchase of new uniforms. One of the legends of the "Red Raiders" name origin comes from 1934, when Tech played in California and a paper referred to them as a "red raiding team."

In 1935, Cawthon generated more notice as he flew his squad to a game in Detroit. In Cawthon's mind, the gambit was a winner for the institution. "This will focus attention on Tech, bring attention to our fine record—in football and scholastically." The stunt did not turn out well, however, as air sickness and delays made most of the players weak, and Tech lost the contest, 37–0.

Successes on the field brought both national attention and controversy. There were concerns about players' time away from class as well as the cost of cross-country trips. Further worries came about because the team played so few games in-conference and because of the use of an ineligible player in the 1939 Cotton Bowl. The 1938 and 1940 teams combined for a mark of 19–1–1, but continued disputes led to Cawthon's resignation in August 1941. He then spent time in the military, coaching professional football, and athletic administration at the University of Alabama. Coach Cawthon died of a heart attack on December 31, 1962.

As noted in a biography of Coach Cawthon, he was a man of his time with "the deeply ingrained prejudices of a Southerner." These traits, and his often-rough treatment of many of his players, would not be acceptable behaviors now, on the field or off. Still, Pete Cawthon is to be recognized as the most successful football coach in school history, one who led the Red Raiders to their first-ever bowl games, as well as their first airplane flight.

Michael Crabtree and Graham Harrell

When Red Raider quarterback Graham Harrell connected with Michael Crabtree on a dramatic game-winning touchdown to beat then-No. 1 Texas 39–33, it meant more to the university and its alumni than just a football game. But it was indeed a great game: ESPN recently ranked it 72nd of the 150 greatest games in college football history.

Striving for recognition

By the time Texas Tech was founded, Texas A&M was already forty-seven years old, and the University of Texas had been around forty years. Even as Texas Tech matured—growing into a world-class university—Red Raiders felt that the older Texas institutions disparaged them. But over a few hours on a field or court you could be equals—or even look down from a position of victory. That's why it was a big deal when Texas Tech was invited into the Southwest Conference in the late 1950s with Texas and Texas A&M.

The game

Jump ahead to November 1, 2008, when all three universities were now in the Big 12 Conference. The stage was set for one of the greatest moments in Texas Tech sports history. The Red Raider football team, undefeated and ranked 7th in the country, was hosting the undefeated No. 1 Longhorns on national television. ESPN's College Game Day made its first visit to Lubbock. Jones AT&T Stadium was packed with tens of thousands dressed in black.

"When you played at Texas Tech, you had to have a chip on your shoulder. A&M and Texas looked down on you and you had something to prove," Harrell said more than a decade later.

The Red Raiders built an early lead, up 22–6 at halftime. Texas cut the lead to 29–19 at the end of three quarters and finally took its first lead of the game, 33–32, with 1:29 to play.

As the Longhorns were driving for the go-ahead score in the south end zone, Harrell watched from the sidelines. If the Longhorns scored, he was thinking, he hoped there would be enough time left to do what his high-powered offense did so well.

"I thought they'd run out the clock. I felt they gave us too much time. I felt pretty confident we had a chance to score," he said. Harrell had experience with comebacks. Two years earlier, he had rallied the Red Raiders from a 31-point deficit to Minnesota in the Insight Bowl to win 44–41 in overtime. His team's chances against Texas got better when Jamar Wall took Texas's kickoff back to the Texas Tech 38.

The drive

The clock showed 1:23 left, 62 yards to the end zone, and Texas Tech had one timeout remaining. All the Red Raiders needed was a field goal, but Harrell wanted a touchdown. It took six plays and, with one exception, it was the same play. Coach Mike Leach called it "Six": two receivers on each side run a vertical pattern down the field. It was called "Six" because if you did it right, you got six points. Harrell also referred to it as "Four Verts." The team could change formations and Harrell would decide who to pass to depending on what the defense was doing—so it could look like different plays.

"Coach Leach always said the play is a suggestion and gave his quarterback the ability to check anywhere on field. He's the only coach who will give his quarterback a ton of freedom and expects you to do your job. That's the whole philosophy of offense. Give you a formation and the ability to change it . . . but you'd better made it work," he said.

Harrell went to work from his own 38. On first down, Harrell hit running back Baron Batch for eight yards and the clock kept running. Detron Lewis—on the only play of the drive that wasn't "Six"—took a screen pass to the 50 for a first down. The clock stopped as the chains moved.

When Harrell took the next snap, there were 41 seconds left. He hit Lewis again for a dozen more yards to the Texas 38 and a pass to Edward Britton got another first down at the Texas 28. When Harrell took the next snap there were 15 seconds left. He scrambled left under pressure and saw Britton on the left side. Harrell threw to Britton, who turned away to block for his quarterback, thinking Harrell was going to run. The ball bounced off Britton's hands and popped softly into the air.

Longhorn Blake Gideon went to corral the ball and for a few seconds almost everyone in Jones AT&T Stadium—and everyone watching on TV—thought Gideon had intercepted the pass, securing Texas's win.

Everybody but Harrell.

"I had the perfect angle. I saw the ball drop straight through [Gideon]," said Harrell. "So I know we've got to get set and run another play. But people were still confused." Once it was clear what happened there were now eight seconds left. Texas Tech still had the timeout if they needed to try a field goal.

The play

Crabtree, who won the Biletnikoff Award as the best receiver in college football the year before and would again, had had a quiet second half. When Harrell took the snap, he quickly decided to pass to Crabtree down the right sideline because the Longhorns didn't put two defenders on him. Their four cornerbacks covered each of the four receivers running the "Verts" and two safeties would help. It was not an easy defense to throw against.

"I thought there was no way they'd let me go to Crabtree. They'd want me to go anywhere but to that big monster," he said. Crabtree sprinted down the sideline and Texas cornerback Curtis Brown followed him with his back to Harrell. Harrell saw his chance and threw toward Crabtree's back shoulder, away from the defender and high enough to get over him. Crabtree turned toward the sideline and caught the ball just in bounds around the 5-yard line as Brown was trying to reach for it.

Brown tried to tackle Crabtree around his chest, but the latter turned away and sprinted into the end zone. Safety Earl Thomas—who later helped the Baltimore Ravens win a Super Bowl—came over to help Brown but ended up in front of the play and not in position to stop Crabtree when he spun away. Harrell at first hoped his teammate would go out of bounds, leaving the Red Raiders with enough time for a game-winning short field goal.

"Crabtree had a better plan," said Harrell, adding that the moment wouldn't have been as good if the Red Raiders kicked a field goal. Crabtree knew he was in bounds and just wanted to get into the end zone and not put pressure on their kicker. ESPN's Chris Fowler, who'd hosted Game Day earlier on campus with his colleagues and special guest Bob Knight, is shown on the sideline with his mouth wide open as Crabtree sprinted away.

For Harrell, "It was a special moment—that year and the game will always be remembered. Coach Leach's whole Texas Tech era all came together."

Images courtesy of Texas Tech Athletics

"I thought there was no way they'd let me go to Crabtree. They'd want me to go anywhere but to that big monster."

"It was a special moment—that year and the game will always be remembered."

Spike Dykes

The sign read "Fire Spike."

It would be hard to blame Tech fans for being pessimistic about their football team's chances on the evening of October 2, 1999, but this seemed to be a low point. As the 5th-ranked Texas A&M Aggies began warmups on the Jones Stadium turf, an individual in the student section raised a sign calling for the ouster of Tech's all-time winningest coach: Spike Dykes.

A widely beloved, grandfatherly sort of character, Dykes was in his thirteenth season as Red Raider head coach in 1999. To members of the national media, Spike personified the hardscrabble grit and authenticity of West Texas itself. At an earlier point in his career, he coached under the Friday Night Lights at Midland's Lee High School, Odessa Permian's chief rival. But times were tough on that October night, and while some may have grumbled about the sign's appropriateness, very few would have questioned its message, especially given what they'd seen on the same field just two weeks prior, when the Red Raiders fell 14–21 to a North Texas team widely considered one of the worst in the country. That loss dropped Spike's career home record against UNT to 0–3, which only made the situation worse.

Roughly four hours later, however, Tech students stormed the field to celebrate one of the biggest upset wins in school history, a 21–19 takedown of their archrivals from College Station. And the Jones Stadium goalposts came down for the first time. That was Red Raider football under Spike Dykes in a nutshell. Never predictable. Never boring.

In his thirteen seasons in Lubbock, Dykes won games he was supposed to lose and lost games he was supposed to win. He retired at the end of the 1999 season as the school's all-time leader in wins, with eighty-two. He also retired as the school's all-time leader in losses, with sixty-seven. A 2008 inductee to the Texas Sports Hall of Fame, Dykes was named Southwest Conference Coach of the Year three times and Big 12 Coach of the year once. In January 1995, he led Tech to their first Cotton Bowl appearance since 1939. He beat Texas six times, more than any other coach in school history. He also beat A&M six times, including five times when the Aggies were ranked in the top 25 (twice in the top 10). With a career home record of 51–24, Spike was instrumental in turning Jones Stadium into "The Jones," a place reputed for its raucous atmosphere and propensity for showcasing the unexpected. For years, the Athletics Department sold football tickets under the slogan, "Tell Spike I'll Be There!"

"Tell Spike . . ." as if you knew him personally. People felt that way about him. He was that kind of man. It's hard to think about Spike Dykes without smiling. He certainly had a way with words, especially when times were tough. Once he explained a loss by saying his team had "played about like three tons of buzzard puke," and later commented, "They say you lose 10 percent of your fan base every year. And I've been here 11 years, so you do the math."

Eulogizing Dykes in 2017, former Longhorns head coach Mack Brown said that Spike Dykes had made him laugh more than anyone he'd ever known. But you don't induct someone into the Texas Sports Hall of Fame simply because they make you laugh. For those who knew Spike, that was just a bonus.

Image courtesy of the Southwest Collection / Special Collections Library

Jim Gaspard

By the time Jim Gaspard got to Texas Tech, he'd seen the world via the US Navy and was four years older than his fellow new students. Gaspard had left the Brooklyn Navy Yard in his 1963 Volvo. He drove down the east coast, stopped in his hometown of Port Arthur, Texas and pulled into Lubbock with a stereo system that could blow someone out of a room. He was ready to learn and get involved. In the process, he created a Texas Tech icon.

Gaspard joined Delta Tau Delta and became a Saddle Tramp. He heard rumblings in a Saddle Tramp officers' meeting that the Southwest Conference was considering banning animal mascots from road football games because fields were getting damaged. It was true that Tech's Masked Rider and horse ripped up grass, but Gaspard felt this was a ploy against the Masked Rider because the other animal mascots didn't run up and down a field. An idea started bouncing around his noggin.

When in the Navy, he'd seen The Famous Chicken mascot at San Diego Padres games and Mickey Mouse and his fellow Disney characters at Disneyland. What if Texas Tech had a mascot that could travel? Gaspard also liked Dirk West's cartoons in the *Lubbock Avalanche-Journal* of a hulking Tech football player. He visited with West, who was in the process of changing the character to the Red Raider, inspired by the Yosemite Sam cartoon. Gaspard quietly started building a mascot in room 242 of Wells Hall with the help of his girlfriend, Dinah, whom he'd met at a Delta party. They started with an old football helmet covered with chicken wire and papier-mâché made from strips of the *Avalanche-Journal* and *University Daily* newspapers. Then, at Texas Tech's theater department, he ran into Ginger Perkins.

"I'm looking for someone to help me make a costume," Gaspard told her.

"Well, I'm the assistant costume designer; can I lend a hand?" she responded.

They got materials from stores around Lubbock and Raider Red was born, flipping the new name of West's evolving character. Gaspard shared his vision with the Saddle Tramps in August 1971, showing pictures of the costume. "What would you think if, at the first pep rally, I ran out on the field with the cheerleaders?" he asked.

A few weeks later, Raider Red made his appearance at the pep rally before the Red Raiders would go to New Orleans to play Tulane. An article in the *Avalanche-Journal* said: "A surprise in the festivities was the appearance of Raider Red, a gun-toting comic strip character that appeared to have walked right out of a Dirk West cartoon. The brightly colored papier-mâché costume will be worn by a Saddle Tramp at the football games." After a couple of appearances, Gaspard turned over the costume to Stan Alcott, who was Raider Red for two seasons.

The Southwest Conference never did ban animal mascots—but Raider Red became a great addition. He could go to away football games when the Masked Rider was not an option, to basketball games and more. Raider Red is still a Saddle Tramp or a High Rider, the women's group formed in 1975. The costume developed over the years and now multiple students wear the costume at hundreds of events a year. Jim and Dinah got married in 1973. Ginger Perkins ended up in the entertainment industry in Hollywood. Dirk West and the West family have been proud of his connection to what's become a national champion mascot.

Top right image courtesy of Texas Tech Communications and Marketing.
Left and bottom right images courtesy of the Southwest Collection /
Special Collections Library

Darvin Ham

On April 3, 2013, a local television reporter in Los Angeles handed then-Lakers assistant coach Darvin Ham a framed photo. With cameras rolling, the reporter asked Ham to describe what he saw. The interview was part of Time Warner Cable SportsNet's running series "Backstage Lakers." For this episode, Ham, standing next to Lakers forward Antawn Jamison, proceeded to describe what Texas Tech fans undoubtedly remember as one of the most legendary moments in Red Raider basketball history. March 17, 1996. Richmond, Virginia. Second Round, East Regional. March Madness.

Ham was one of four senior starters on what may have been the best team in school history; with four future NBA players on the roster, it was, at the very least, its most talented. Under the leadership of head coach James Dickey, the Red Raiders went 30–2 during the 1995–96 season, winning the Southwest Conference regular season title (finishing with a perfect 14–0 conference record), before winning the SWC tournament and earning a #3 seed in the East Regional. After a narrow first-round win, Tech squared off against the North Carolina Tar Heels and legendary head coach, Dean Smith. Roughly midway through the first half, with the score tied at 16, Tech forward Jason Sasser missed a five-foot hook shot off the back iron. Cutting through the middle of the lane, Ham soared past UNC forward Antawn Jamison and seven-foot-three-inch center Serge Zwikker, grabbed the rebound in mid-air, and threw down a slam dunk that shattered the backboard into a thousand pieces. Tech never looked back, channeling the momentum from Ham's slam into a 92–73 blowout win and the school's first trip to the Sweet Sixteen in twenty years.

As Ham and Jamison explained for "Backstage Lakers" cameras in 2013, one of those backboard glass shards landed on Jamison's right forearm, leaving a scar and a permanent reminder of one of college basketball's greatest moments.

Tech fans undoubtedly smiled when Ham pointed out Jamison's scar for L.A. TV watchers, but likely not as much as they did, and still do, when they see the March 25, 1996, cover of *Sports Illustrated* picturing Ham under a shower of broken glass—the first time an active Red Raider was featured on the iconic magazine's cover.

It's difficult to think of Darvin Ham without thinking about that moment. But as much as one shattered backboard has meant to Tech fans over the years, Ham's life has been about so much more. In 2003, he and his wife, Denietra—also a Tech grad—founded Urban Youth Development, an organization dedicated to education and "life skills" teaching for disadvantaged kids. Twenty years and hundreds of kids later, Ham's impact on American youth is profound. And in the spirit of practicing what he preaches, Ham returned to Lubbock in 2019, not as a basketball star but as a proud college graduate, completing a bachelor's degree in university studies.

Fans love the image of Ham shattering a backboard, but watching him walk across the stage at United Supermarkets Arena—a building that likely would not have existed without him—was on another level. Darvin Ham. NBA champion. Youth mentor. College graduate.

Fans can now add another accolade to that list: head coach. In 2022, Ham was named the 28th head coach of the Los Angeles Lakers, earning a top coaching spot with one of the NBA's most storied franchises. Ham's hire was cheered by all of Red Raider Nation, of course, but also immediately lending his support was one particularly high-profile figure: superstar LeBron James. Clearly Ham has many other successes still to come in his standout career.

Images courtesy of Texas Tech Athletics

Ham was one of four senior starters on what may have been the best team in school history; with four future NBA players on the roster, it was, at the very least, its most talented.

Danny Hardaway

On February 14, 1967, Danny Hardaway, who graduated high school in Lawton, Oklahoma, became the first African American student to receive an athletic scholarship to Texas Tech University. This came fifteen years after the University of Arizona challenged Texas Tech's policy of excluding African American athletes from playing in games at the TTU stadium. That December, the Board of Directors ruled that African Americans would be allowed to participate in intercollegiate athletics and opened up the football stadium for an all-star African American game. Ann Bryan, the associate editor of the school newspaper, *The Toreador*, praised this decision: "While it is a rather feeble and very belated step toward greater democratic operation of our school, it is at least a step. We are at last beginning to break away from the bigoted, intolerant, binding Jim Crow laws to which the majority of Texas institutions and individuals conform."

Danny Hardaway was an accomplished high school athlete: he had lettered one year in baseball, three in football, three in track and field, and four in basketball. He was co-captain of the football team, made all-district football and basketball, all-region, all-state, and all-American honors, and was named Oklahoma's Outstanding Lineman—all while being ranked twelfth in his graduating class and having served as president of the sophomore class. Hardaway received thirty-eight scholarship offers for football and ten for basketball. He chose Texas Tech.

Hardaway became a student at Texas Tech just six years after Lucille Sugar Barton Graves made history as the first African American student admitted to Texas Tech in summer 1961. He knew what it meant to be the first African American to receive an athletics scholarship. He knew what it meant to make history. In an interview with the school newspaper, Hardaway admitted that he had some initial doubts. "I was hesitant at first, but I didn't let it bother me," he said. And many of his coaches—J. T. King, Burl Bartlett, Bob Bass, Corky Oglesby, and Jess Stiles—were essential in ensuring that his experience was a positive one. In a February 2011 *Lubbock Avalanche-Journal* article on Hardaway's return to Texas Tech as part of the Black History Month program, Hardaway noted, "Those guys really led in making sure that I was protected and made [it] as smooth a transition as possible." He continued, "If it weren't for them, and also some of the kids I met, I probably couldn't have made it. I went through hell, but I caught more hell when we went to other schools. My teammates, almost all of them, really protected me and sheltered me from all that stuff when we were at home."

Hardaway continued to make history. He was an outstanding football player, leading the field in rushing yards and passes. He played for three years as a wide receiver, running back, and halfback at Texas Tech before transferring to Cameron University back in his hometown his senior year because of changes to the offense that would have precluded his playing. But he did more than play football at Texas Tech. He was a charter member of the Student Organization for Unity and Leadership (SOUL), the university's first African American student organization. By 1979, SOUL was renamed the Student Organization for Black Unity (SOBU) and had grown to seventy-five members. Danny Hardaway advocated for educational equity and was not only a voice but an actor for change and justice.

On February 14, 1967, Danny Hardaway became the first African American student to receive an athletic scholarship to Texas Tech University.

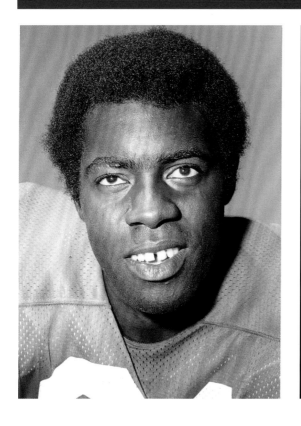

Danny Hardaway advocated for educational equity and was not only a voice but an actor for change and justice.

E. J. Holub

When Texas Tech fans tuned in to Super Bowls LIV and LV, they were pulling for victory by the Kansas City Chiefs, quarterbacked by Patrick Mahomes. These two title games were not the first in which Red Raiders had an alum playing for that team in the NFL's title tilt. On two previous occasions the main focus of interest was on the play of E. J. "The Beast" Holub.

Holub was born on January 5, 1938, in Schulenburg, Texas, but grew up in Lubbock, attending Lubbock High School and competing in the discus and shot put, as well as football, for the Westerners. Upon graduation in 1957 he accepted a scholarship at Texas Tech, where he would go on to become one of the greatest players ever to don the Red Raiders' colors.

He was a real "throwback" to an era when gridiron warriors were expected to play on both sides of the ball. Holub, the epitome of toughness, played both center and linebacker. He would go on to earn second team All-American in 1959 and first team in 1960 as a center. He loved the contact and considered himself a "raw-boned, big gangly kid. We were just a bunch of West Texas cowboys and farm boys who liked to play some football." The fact that he endured more than a dozen surgeries on his knees between the end of his high school and throughout his professional career certainly attest to his passion for the sport.

With the then-separate AFL and NFL leagues seeking to establish teams in Dallas, both the Texans and the Cowboys selected Holub after his graduation from Tech in 1961. He decided to cast his fate with the AFL Texans, who soon moved to Kansas City and became the Chiefs, and was part of three championship teams for the Texans / Chiefs in 1962, 1966, and the league's final season, in 1969. In those early years with Kansas City, it was not uncommon for Holub to line up more than fifty-five of the sixty minutes of contests.

He played in the first-ever Super Bowl, between Kansas City and Green Bay, then again in 1969 versus Minnesota. While the Chiefs lost the first contest against the Packers, they won Super Bowl IV against the Vikings, 23–7. In both contests, Holub played both offense and defense, a feat that has never been repeated. Holub retired just before the start of the 1971 campaign (after another injury). One final tribute to his toughness can be seen in the fact that, even after all the knee surgeries, he was still acclaimed as 2nd team All Pro in the AFL's final year.

Not surprisingly, there were myriad tributes after his playing days. He has the honor of being the first Red Raider to have his number (55) retired (in 1977). He is also a member of various Halls of Fame: Texas Tech, Kansas City Chiefs, National Collegiate, and the Southwest Conference. Lastly, he was inducted into the Tech Ring of Honor in 2013. E. J. Holub passed away from natural causes on September 21, 2019.

Kliff Kingsbury

A photo of Kingsbury and Britney Spears together on the pop star's tour bus in 2002 went viral. So did a photo of him partying with Tom Brady and Mike Tyson at the Kentucky Derby in 2014. A photo of him sitting on his coach in Arizona became one of the most talked-about images of the 2020 NFL Draft, drawing comparisons to something straight out of MTV's *Cribs*. Alex Trebek once read his name in a *Jeopardy!* clue about celebrity look-alikes and Hollywood movie stars.

He also started Spike Dykes' last game as head football coach at Texas Tech. And Mike Leach's first. He played for Bill Belichick in New England. And coached under Art Briles in Houston. He was directly responsible for Johnny Manziel's Heisman Trophy at Texas A&M in 2012. And he discovered, mentored, and introduced the world to Patrick Mahomes.

For three seasons, Kliff Kingsbury commanded Texas Tech's famed "Air Raid" offense, leaving after the 2002 season as the best quarterback in school history and its all-time leader in career passing yards and touchdown passes, with additional records for most passing yards and touchdown passes in a single season and single game. In his final game he earned MVP honors for leading Tech to a 55–15 throttling of Clemson in the 2002 Tangerine Bowl, after which he conducted the Goin' Band as it played "The Matador Song."

Kingbury's greatest contribution to Texas Tech may have come in December 2012 when he took the stage at United Spirit Arena as his alma mater's new head football coach, less than three years after Mike Leach's controversial firing and less than one week after Tommy Tuberville snuck out of the 50 Yard Line steakhouse in Lubbock, abandoning three recruits (and the entire school) to take the head coaching job at the University of Cincinnati. To say the Tech fan base was in an emotionally fragile state at that point would have been an understatement. Kingsbury understood that, and he understood what the Red Raider Nation needed to hear: "One thing I wanted to ask Mr. Hocutt [TTU director of athletics] is if there's any way we can get Cincinnati on the schedule next year." The fans in attendance erupted.

Kliff got it. He was, and always will be, a Red Raider. He talked about "swagger" and having a chip on your shoulder. He knew the fan base needed to be reunified, and brazenly challenging the recently departed and deeply disliked Tuberville did the trick. Local merchandise stores began selling t-shirts that said "Schedule Cincinnati." One year later, after an exciting first season and a triumph over Arizona State in the Holiday Bowl, Tech sold out Jones Stadium for the entire season, a first in school history.

Winning consistently in the highly competitive Big 12 turned out to be a greater challenge than hoped. Kingsbury's tenure as Tech head coach ended following the 2018 season, but the setback was only temporary; less than one month after leaving Tech, Kliff Kingsbury was named head coach of the NFL's Arizona Cardinals.

In so many ways, Kliff Kingsbury embodied much of what people love about Texas Tech. His teams were not always great, but he mixed swagger and style with a commitment to doing things the right way. Red Raiders love their football, and you can't tell the story of Texas Tech football without mentioning Kliff Kingsbury.

Image courtesy of Texas Tech Athletics

Red Raiders love their football, and you can't tell the story of Texas Tech football without mentioning Kliff Kingsbury.

Sally Kipyego

She won nine individual national championships in track and field, more than any other woman in the history of the sport. She was the first athlete ever to win four NCAA championships in a single year. She was also the first Kenyan to win an individual NCAA championship in cross-country. She may even be the greatest female college athlete of all time.

For Sally Kipyego, one run will always stand out above the rest.

When Kipyego was only 11 years old she saw a friend suffer massive head trauma, the result of a bicycle accident. Virtually alone in the Kenyan countryside, with the friend in desperate need of emergency medical care, Kipyego sprinted seven miles to the nearest village in search of a doctor. She found one, but he was drunk and refused to help. With no other options, Kipyego ran back to the scene of the accident—covering the same seven miles—arriving just in time to watch her friend die.

"You lose something when something like that happens," Kipyego once explained to a reporter at ESPN. "It's kind of haunted me to look back at that during the rest of my life. My country was very poor, and the health care wasn't good. . . . I'd like to see if I can help change those things."

Running was always a means to an end for Sally Kipyego. Whether it was the only way she could find a doctor or get to school—or get to an American university—Kipyego's feet took her where she needed to go. Eventually, those feet carried her to West Texas and the Texas Tech track and field/cross-country program, under the mentorship of coaches like Jon Murray and the legendary Wes Kittley. Under that tutelage, Kipyego made a name for herself in the national (and international) world of track and field from 2006 to 2009, becoming one of the most decorated athletes in NCAA history.

As she ran on the track, she also made the rounds in local hospitals on her way to a degree from Texas Tech University's School of Nursing. "She's like a Mother Teresa," a teammate of Kipyego's told *Runner's World* magazine in 2011. "She is very spiritual and warm and channels optimism and positivity like a direct beam from above to the very spot where she stands. It's like there is a spotlight from heaven following her around, charming her life and those who come into contact with her."

"Red Raiders far and wide are so proud of what she has accomplished," Kittley remarked to *USA Today*, after Kipyego qualified for the 2020 US Olympic team at the age of 34, just three years after becoming a US citizen in 2017 and eight years after winning bronze for her native Kenya at the 2012 Olympic Games in London.

In 2019, Texas Tech won its first overall national championship in track and field after Kittley's men's team dominated the competition at the NCAA outdoor meet in Austin. At that time, the track program was a national power. Other than Kittley, few individuals played a bigger part in that transformation than Sally Kipyego. Yet at the end of the day, Kipyego's biggest mark on the world may come thanks to the training she received at the TTU School of Nursing.

Images courtesy of Texas Tech Athletics

Kipyego made a name for herself in the national (and international) world of track and field from 2006 to 2009, becoming one of the most decorated athletes in NCAA history.

Patrick Mahomes

In the midst of a global pandemic, political strife, and widespread economic uncertainty and social anxiety, Patrick Mahomes carried the Kansas City Chiefs to the Super Bowl for the first time in fifty years, was named MVP of that game, became the first-ever starting quarterback from a Texas college to win a Super Bowl, signed the most lucrative contract in the history of the NFL, got engaged to his high school sweetheart, became a father, bought a share in a Major League Baseball franchise, became the first Kansas City Chief to ever grace the cover of the iconic "Madden NFL" video game, and was named to *Time* magazine's list of 100 most influential people on Earth—all while parlaying his success into several national endorsement deals, growing a nonprofit foundation dedicated to health and wellness for impoverished children, and using his voice to promote causes of racial and social justice.

And that was just 2020.

No Texas Tech alumnus has ever matched the level of national and international fame Mahomes achieved in his first few years in the NFL. The son of a former professional baseball player, he's never appeared on a stage that seemed too big for him. In one of his first plays as Texas Tech quarterback, he fumbled the ball, recovered his own fumble, and threw a last-ditch pass midair while he was being tackled. It was intercepted, yes, but the pass did hit his receiver in the hands.

From that point forward, over the next two-and-a-half seasons Mahomes became a legend. He threw ninety-three touchdown passes against only twenty-four interceptions, accumulating more than 11,000 yards in the air, including 734 in a 2016 match against Oklahoma. He ran for an additional eighty-five yards in that game, giving him the NCAA record for total yards in one game at 819. When he was a sophomore in 2015, Mahomes's Red Raiders ranked second in the country in total offense; one year later, as a junior, his offense was number one—the best of the nation's best.

Unfortunately for Mahomes—and for all Red Raider football fans—Texas Tech's 2015 defense was, statistically, the second worst in the country. In 2016, it was the very worst. In his two full seasons as starting quarterback, Mahomes-led teams went 12–13, including eight losses in which his offense scored thirty-five points or more. In four of those, the Red Raiders scored more than fifty. Nevertheless, Patrick Mahomes will always be one of the most popular athletes to ever come out of Texas Tech. And perhaps, of all the images associated with this phenomenal talent, the ones Red Raider fans may have enjoyed the most were those of Mahomes and his Chiefs teammate, Travis Kelce, cheering on the Red Raider basketball team at the 2019 Final Four, just one of the crowd, yelling like everyone else.

"Voice gone," Mahomes tweeted after the basketball team's 61–51 win over Michigan State in the national semifinal. Gone for one night, perhaps. But at only 27 years of age on Texas Tech's centennial, chances are that Patrick's voice will be heard for years to come.

Images courtesy of Texas Tech Athletics

Jeannine McHaney

Recruited from Arkansas State University in 1966 by Drs. Mary Dabney and Margaret Wilson, Jeannine McHaney began her career at Texas Tech as an assistant professor in the Department of Health, Physical Education and Recreation. That same year she was appointed the Women's Intramural Director and given a measly annual budget of $500 to run the program, which existed in large part due to the women's coaches contributing their time for free. Jeannine herself served as volleyball and gymnastics coach.

With the enactment of Title IX, McHaney was appointed the school's first Women's Athletic Director in 1975, a role she fiercely took on to expand upon and improve the women's athletic program. During her 10-year term in that role, McHaney grappled with gender disparity issues in the areas of sorely inadequate funding and second-rate facilities for the women's athletic teams. Despite such difficulties, her efforts gained momentum. In 1982, she hired Lockney High School basketball coach Marsha Sharp, a momentous decision which eleven years later netted Texas Tech its first national championship win. Sharp, incidentally, credits McHaney as being one of the most influential individuals in her coaching career.

When the men's and women's athletic departments were combined in 1985, McHaney was appointed assistant athletics director, then promoted in 1991 to associate director of athletics. Over the course of her twenty-eight years with the university, McHaney was heavily involved with and influential in women's athletics in both the Southwest Conference and the NCAA. Among her many recognitions was being named the 1993 Administrator of the Year by the Women's Basketball Coaches Association.

While she lost her decade-long struggle with cancer in October 1994, many reminders of the significant contributions McHaney made at Texas Tech remain. The High Riders spirit organization created an award in her name, and there is an endowed graduate athlete scholarship named after her in the Department of Kinesiology and Sports Management.

In addition to her becoming the first woman inducted into the Texas Tech Hall of Honor, the Board of Regents, in May 2002, approved naming part of the Hall of Honor section at the west entrance area of the United Spirit Arena as the Jeannine McHaney Hall of Honor (with the other half being named after Polk Robison). A bronze sculpture of McHaney by artist Rosie Sandifer was dedicated on January 17, 2004. It was placed in the Hall of Honor with a plaque containing a heartfelt quote by Lady Raider Noel Johnson following Tech's 1993 NCAA tournament championship that affirms, "Any success in the past or future of women's athletics at Texas Tech is a result of Jeannine McHaney. Her courage and leadership will forever be embedded in Texas Tech athletics." The National Association of Collegiate Women Athletics Administrators recognized McHaney posthumously in 2006 as a Lifetime Achievement Award recipient. Moreover, Texas Tech softball began hosting the Jeannine McHaney Memorial Classic, named in honor of the school's architect of women's athletics, beginning in 2010.

Men's Basketball 2019 Final Four Team

Norense Odiase and Tariq Owens. One on one. As it got more intense, the trash-talking kicked in.

"Your hands are not fast enough for this game," Odiase told Owens.

They were playing foosball. The testosterone-laden show-down took place at the Bachelor Party Olympics in summer 2021. The duo from the 2019 Red Raider basketball team that came within seconds of winning a national title were cele-brating the upcoming wedding of teammate Andrew Sorrells. Besides Odiase, Owens, and the groom, Matt Mooney, Jarrett Culver—plus Keenan Evans from the 2018 team—joined other guys at a rented house in Scottsdale. Davide Moretti couldn't make the bachelor party due to COVID travel restrictions.

At the house, the guys were split into four teams and competed in pickleball, a relay race, darts, billiards, paintball, foosball—and hoops. Their competitive fire, which drove the 2019 squad to the final game of the year against Virginia at the US Bank Stadium in Minneapolis, had not diminished. Sorrells saw something different in that team compared to his previous seasons: a chemistry creating a strong bond.

"We wanted to win bad and were going to do whatever it took. There was nobody we had to worry about their com-mitment level. Every player on that team would make 300 shots a day and that was not mandatory. Everybody would get in an extra workout," he said, adding that the coaches didn't have to crack the whip. Odiase, in his senior year, was the leader, which came naturally. Owens and Mooney were transfers who arrived in Lubbock with chips on their shoul-ders and attitude. This was their last chance. Then add in Lubbock's Culver, who after the season realized his dreams of playing in the National Basketball Association.

Texas Tech basketball had captured the national spotlight after reaching the Elite Eight the first time in school history the previous year under coach Chris Beard. His 2019 team started 15–1, the only loss coming to then-No. 2 Duke in New York's Madison Square Garden. Then the Red Raiders lost three straight Big 12 Conference games in January.

"We had some tough practices and we had to look at ourselves in the mirror. The way it was going wasn't going to get it done," said Sorrells. They finished the regular season 11–1, including destroying Kansas 91–62 at home as United Supermarkets Arena shook from a packed house and the Raider Riot—the wild student section that rivaled the best in the country. "Everybody was focused, and we were clicking on all cylinders," said Sorrells.

After an early exit in the Big 12 Tournament, the Red Raiders beat Northern Kentucky, Buffalo, Michigan, top-seed Gonzaga, and Michigan State in the NCAA Tournament by an average of 14 points before losing to Virginia 85–77 in overtime. After the national championship loss, the locker room was quiet, punctuated by tears. "I'd never seen these guys cry," said Sorrells. "It was so emotional. We were up three with 19 seconds to go and it slipped away."

A year after that loss, the team virtually gathered for what was supposed to be a half-hour Zoom call. Their bond contin-ues to this day, playing out through a bustling group text and shared support over basketball, family, and career milestones.

"Everybody knows what's going on in each other's lives. It's a family," said Sorrells.

Images courtesy of Texas Tech Athletics

Corky Oglesby

Corky Oglesby could make anyone laugh, even when the topic of conversation was his own terminal pancreatic cancer diagnosis in summer 2017. "He had me laughing for about thirty minutes," one former athlete said of the conversation he had with Oglesby about his cancer. "I was laughing so hard, my sides hurt." Oglesby—or simply "Corky," as everyone called him—was just that kind of guy.

Not everyone gets to attend their own "celebration of life" event, let alone do so in front of nearly a thousand people. But not everyone is Corky Oglesby, which is why Red Raiders far and wide gathered at the City Bank Coliseum on August 5, 2017, to share stories and laughs with a former track and field coach whom Wes Kittley described as a pioneer, a friend, and a "blessing."

"I don't mean to hurt anybody's feelings, but there's been nobody more underappreciated than this man right here," Kittley told the Coliseum crowd that day. "Corky Oglesby's an icon. Corky Oglesby *is* Texas Tech." Sadly, Corky's fight with cancer ended a few months later, on November 19, 2017. He was 81 years old and had spent the last forty-eight years of his life in Lubbock, first arriving in 1969 as Tech's new assistant basketball coach. For the next six years, Corky was responsible for recruiting some of the best basketball players of that era, including many of the first African American student-athletes in school history, one of whom turned out to be future Ring of Honor inductee, Rick Bullock.

Corky left the basketball program in 1975 to become head coach of track and field. He led that program for the next the twenty-one years, becoming the longest-serving head coach in school history until Wes Kittley surpassed the mark in 2022. After leaving the track program in 1995, he spent the next two decades working for the Red Raider Club, building relationships with current students, future students, parents, faculty, staff, and alumni; everyone in Red Raider Nation got to know Corky at one point or another. And he seemed to love every minute of it.

"I told him one day when he wasn't feeling good, 'You ought to go home,'" recalled Kent Hance on the day of Corky's passing. "He said, 'I don't want to go home. I want to be at the Red Raider Club with my friends.'" Corky's legend continued to grow in the years after his death. On January 13, 2018, Kittley's track program hosted the inaugural "Corky Classic" at Texas Tech's brand-new, state-of-the-art, $48 million Sports Performance Center, just south of Jones AT&T Stadium. Less than a year later, Corky was posthumously inducted into the Texas Track and Field Coaches Association Hall of Fame. And, of course, no Red Raider will ever be able to relive highlights of the Red Raider basketball team's first-ever trip to the Elite Eight (in 2018) without noticing the word "CORKY" emblazoned on the left shoulder of each player's jersey.

In 2019, Kittley's track program also acknowledged Corky's contributions after claiming the school's first-ever national championship in a men's sport. "Corky Oglesby is a legend," Director of Athletics Kirby Hocutt once reflected on his departed friend. "He in so many ways demonstrated what being a Red Raider is all about."

Images courtesy of Texas Tech Athletics

> **"Corky Oglesby's an icon. Corky Oglesby *is* Texas Tech."**

Gabriel Rivera

He became a household name by using his freakishly quick 6-foot-2-inch, 300-pound body to sack quarterbacks on the football field. But he spent the last fifteen years of his life using his wheelchair-bound voice to help some of the poorest kids in Texas.

Gabriel Rivera is without a doubt one of the greatest football players in Texas Tech history, perhaps one of the best defensive players of all time. A consensus first-team All-American in 1982, a first-round pick of the Pittsburgh Steelers in 1983, a member of the Southwest Conference's All-Decade team for the 1980s, and a 2012 inductee into the College Football Hall of Fame, Rivera was a monster at defensive tackle, earning what might be the greatest nickname in the history of college football: "Señor Sack." After one particularly memorable performance against the top-ranked Washington Huskies in 1982, legendary coach Don James called Rivera "the best defensive player I've seen." One Lubbock sportswriter described Rivera as a "mad hornet trapped in a fast-moving car." The Pittsburgh Steelers thought so much of Rivera that they drafted him to replace NFL Hall of Famer "Mean" Joe Greene, selecting the Texas Tech standout instead of hometown quarterback and future NFL Hall of Famer Dan Marino. Rivera's future seemed bright.

Tragically, everything changed on October 20, 1983, when Rivera slammed his car into another vehicle while driving through a Pittsburgh suburb after practice. The accident left Rivera a lifelong paraplegic.

Several years later, Rivera—who also suffered significant memory loss as a result of the accident—recalled the long aftermath of that day as a season of anger and frustration. Thankfully, however, with the support of his wife and children, Rivera found an outlet for those frustrations, reconnecting with his hometown of San Antonio through SATX Inner City Development Center, a nonprofit organization dedicated to serving one of the city's poorest neighborhoods. After a period of wandering through his own personal wilderness, Rivera spent much of the last two decades of his life preaching against the evils of drunk driving, while at the same time living out Inner City Development Center's stated mission to "lift the dignity of the individual." He loved the kids he tutored there, and they loved and respected him, often noting Rivera's transparent honesty and the credibility his words carried.

In September 2014, Texas Tech inducted Rivera into its highly exclusive Ring of Honor at Jones AT&T Stadium. "When I first got injured, I had hope that I would walk again," Rivera said at the time. "I still have hope, but now I just live my life and keep going. . . . I enjoy life. Do the best with the life you have."

Gabriel Rivera died less than four years later. He was only 57 years old. His life may not have been long, nor did it include a successful NFL career. But if you ask his family, or the dozens of kids whose lives were shaped through Inner City Development, there is no question that Rivera left a powerful legacy. He may have become famous for knocking people down, but it was his ability to lift and restore dignity to the disadvantaged that truly changed the world.

Top left: Gabe getting pointers from Texas and Steelers legend "Mean" Joe Greene. Image courtesy of the Southwest Collection / Special Collections Library.
Top right: Image courtesy of Sean Cunningham, who is pictured here as a little boy. Cunningham is now a professor in the History Department at Texas Tech.
Bottom left: Gabe thwarting an attempted block by an Air Force Academy fullback. Image courtesy of the Southwest Collection / Special Collections Library.

Gabriel Rivera is without a doubt one of the greatest football players in Texas Tech history, perhaps one of the best defensive players of all time.

Polk Robison

Polk Robison was a legendary Texas Tech athlete, coach, and administrator. He was a well-dressed, well-spoken gentleman who played by the rules—even if not everyone saw that as a virtue. It was Texas Tech coaching legend Berl Huffman who used to complain about the high ethical standards Robison held. He would say, "Tech will never really be an athletic power as long as Polk Robison's Athletic Director because he's too damn honest."

Robison lived a long and honest life, dying in 2008 at the age of 96. He was born in Tennessee but came to Lubbock with his family and graduated from Lubbock High School.

At Tech, with the 6-foot, 2-inch Robison at center, the then-Matadors won three Border Conference basketball titles before he graduated with a journalism degree in 1934. "He was very proud of his English and worked very hard to ensure his children and eventual in-laws—like me—were quite correct in their use of the English language," said Huffman's son, referring to the old coach's habit of complaining about the honest Robison. "He was a precise gentlemanly fellow. If you met him, you'd probably say he was an English professor, not a basketball coach."

Robison led Tech's basketball team from the early 1940s to the early 1960s, culminating in the Southwest Conference title after a 63–60 victory over Texas in Lubbock's Memorial Coliseum in 1961. It was Tech's first SWC title in any sport. Contributing to Tech's propulsion into the SWC was all the Border Conference titles Robison brought to Lubbock. The night of the SWC title, Robison was mobbed by players and fans before addressing the crowd, an example of how accessible he was, said Huffman. "When he was Athletic Director, the Athletic Department was wide open. You could walk in there and have a cup of coffee with the Athletic Director.

He'd sit down and talk to you. He never felt like he was above anyone else," said Huffman.

Robison also recruited Borger hoops star Gerald Myers—who, like Robison, went on to be a Red Raider player, coach, and athletic director. But not without a fight, said Huffman.

Myers had accepted a scholarship offer from Tech, but legendary Oklahoma State coach Hank Iba lured Myers to Stillwater. "Coach Robison found out, drove to Stillwater, went in the dorm, packed up Gerald's stuff, and brought him back to Lubbock. I guess you would say he was simply trying to enforce an agreement Gerald had made. And he turned out to be one of Coach Robison's great friends and admirers," said Huffman. Robison also tried to recruit a player out of Amarillo named T. Boone Pickens, who eventually ended up going to Oklahoma State.

When Robison retired from Tech in 1977, he'd spent forty-one years of his life at the university during its first fifty-one years. Coach Robison stayed fit and healthy well into his 90s. He'd visit friends in the Carillon retirement community a few days a week, and Huffman asked his father-in-law why he didn't move there. "There's just too many old people out there," Robison told him. One day, Walt and Anne Huffman were driving to his house on 28th Street. Robison was using a push mower to do his lawn and was smoking a cigar. "I wish you'd tell him to quit smoking those cigars," Anne told Walt. Walt responded: "He's 92 years old and out here on his own with a push mower. I don't think I'm going to tell him anything about that cigar. In fact, I'm thinking about picking it up myself."

Bottom right: Group portrait of the basketball team with their coaches, Gene Gibson and Polk Robison, taken in 1960.
Images courtesy of the Southwest Collection / Special Collections Library

"He was a precise gentlemanly fellow. If you met him, you'd probably say he was an English professor, not a basketball coach."

John Scovell

John Scovell grew up in Dallas, the son of Field Scovell, a businessman who was also "Mr. Cotton Bowl" and who played a role in bringing the Dallas Cowboys to the Metroplex. John—and later, his three sons—grew up meeting some of the biggest names in sports and business in America. But they didn't develop big egos, partly because humility is valued in the Scovell family and from the Texas Tech imprint on John and his boys, who all played football for the Red Raiders. "West Texas starts to rub off on you. It starts to remind you you're not as important as you think you are—a way of creating a little bit of humility which we could all use more of," said Dupree Scovell.

John's dad played football for Texas A&M almost 100 years ago. John grew up in Aggie gear but decided to play football for Texas Tech. "Texas Tech was interested in me. I got the feeling A&M wanted Field Scovell's son and that was the difference," said John. John played quarterback for coach J. T. King. In 1967, he led the Red Raiders to their first Southwest Conference win over Texas, 19–13, in Austin. The plane flying back to Lubbock couldn't land because the runway was filled with happy fans. "This was going to be our great return and we were practicing how we'd wave," said John. The plane was diverted to Amarillo before the team eventually got to Lubbock, but by then the crowd had dispersed.

John's oldest son, Field III, followed his dad to Texas Tech. "I wanted to be part of what my dad was part of," he said. Field played receiver for Spike Dykes, who became one of three men he called on Father's Day along with John and his freshman basketball coach. He was on the field when Sammy Morris turned a play called 26 bootleg throwback into an 81-yard touchdown to beat his grandfather's Aggies in College Station. Field became an orthopedic surgeon and Texas Tech team doctor before eventually moving back to the Metroplex. During his last year in Lubbock, he worked with the Red Raider basketball team that made a run to the Elite Eight in the NCAA playoffs.

Brothers King and Dupree followed Field to Tech. They were receivers in the Air Raid offense's early years. Dupree got four bachelor's degrees from Tech and was the first Tech grad to go to Stanford's graduate school. King and Dupree joined their father's company, Woodbine, which focuses on real estate investment, development, and management.

John went on to serve as a Texas Tech University System regent, and the family launched the Scovell Business Leadership Program at the Rawls College of Business. "We were raised to appreciate what you get and return the favor," said King. "We got so much out of Tech: a job, something to root for, my best friends. It's given my kids something to root for and be proud of."

Diane Scovell, John's wife, has a rich Texas Tech history as well. Her mother went to Tech, her brother was a Masked Rider, and Diane was a twirler who caught John's eye. Among them, John, Field III, King, and Dupree scored twenty-one touchdowns for the Red Raiders in their careers. But Diane likes to remind them that she spent more time in the end zone than all of them put together when she was twirling.

Images courtesy of the Scovell family

John went on to serve as a Texas Tech University System regent, and the family launched the Scovell Business Leadership Program at the Rawls College of Business.

Sheryl Swoopes

A collegiate national champion, a three-time Olympic gold medalist, a four-time WNBA champion and three-time league MVP, a member of the James Naismith Memorial Basketball Hall of Fame, and the first woman to have a Nike shoe named in her honor—the "Air Swoopes"—it's no wonder she's often described as "the female Michael Jordan." She even named her son Jordan. Sheryl Swoopes's legacy includes far more than simply her success on the basketball court, which is why ESPN chose to document her story in its influential "Nine for IX" film series in 2013, celebrating the resilience, endurance, success, and legacy of women in sports.

Tech fans obviously remember Swoopes first and foremost as the best women's basketball player in school history. A native of Brownfield, Texas, Swoopes left Lubbock with too many legendary performances to count, foremost among those being her 50-point outburst against Texas in the 1993 Southwest Conference tournament championship game at Reunion Arena in Dallas, as well as her record-setting 47-point performance against Ohio State in the NCAA national championship game in Atlanta just a few weeks later.

After leading Team USA to a gold medal in that same city in 1996, Swoopes became the first player ever to sign a contract with the brand-new Women's National Basketball Association, inking a deal with the Houston Comets. She was, in fact, the centerpiece of the upstart league's marketing campaign, which is what made her unexpected pregnancy that year so "inconvenient" to league owners. Having a baby forced Swoopes to miss most of the WNBA's inaugural season. She returned to the floor just weeks after giving birth to her son, the aforementioned Jordan, and even spent a few halftimes breastfeeding her child before playing the second half. Nevertheless, "Mama" Swoopes, as teammates and players would call her over the coming years, was all business on the court; the Houston Comets won the WNBA championship in summer 1997. And did it again in 1998. And 1999. And 2000.

In 2005, at the age of 34, Swoopes made headlines again, first by winning her third WNBA Most Valuable Player award, then by becoming "the first high-profile African American basketball player to come out as gay." "I was waiting to exhale," Swoopes told reporters upon making the announcement. "I was at a point in my life where I am just tired of having to pretend to be somebody I am not." But in making that announcement, Swoopes also insisted that she had not been born gay, a point that raised eyebrows in the LGBTQ community, as did her subsequent engagement to a male friend in 2011. The couple married in 2017. "I'm in love with whom I am supposed to be in love with," she told *ESPN The Magazine*. As one reporter put it, Swoopes was "not a spokeswoman, not a contrarian, just herself."

A trailblazer off the court and a Texas Tech basketball legend, Sheryl Swoopes is who she is. Just herself.

Tech fans obviously remember Swoopes first and foremost as the best women's basketball player in school history.

Tim Tadlock

"It wasn't too long ago that a guy told me that Texas Tech can't go to Omaha. Well, guess what? We're about to find out." That was Tim Tadlock, on June 8, 2012, during his introductory press conference as the ninth head coach in Red Raider baseball history. Nine years later—after three conference championships and four trips to the College World Series—Texas Tech rewarded Tadlock with a lifetime contract, making it clear to everyone in the college baseball world that the Red Raiders had grown fond of their visits to Omaha and had no intention of ending those trips any time soon.Texas Tech became a nationally recognized baseball powerhouse under Tim Tadlock. But for most of its existence the program was little more than a local afterthought. The school fielded its first team in 1926 but eliminated the program at the end of the 1929 season. It did not field another team until 1954, although success continued to elude the school for another three decades. Then came Larry Hays.

As head coach from 1987 to 2008, Hays changed the face of Tech baseball. In 1995, he achieved the program's first conference championship, then came within one strike of Omaha, losing back-to-back heartbreakers to Stanford in the NCAA Regional. Still, the program reached unprecedented heights during Hays' twenty-two seasons in the dugout, including two conference championships, one conference tournament championship, and nine NCAA tournament appearances. As it turned out, Hays' greatest accomplishment may have been the recruitment of a junior-college transfer shortstop in 1991: Tim Tadlock.

After helping the Red Raiders to its first-ever 40-win season in 1991, Tadlock graduated from Tech in 1992. He launched his coaching career the next year. By the end of the decade, Tadlock was a national figure in the world of college baseball, having led Grayson Junior College to consecutive national championships in 1999 and 2000. From Grayson, Tadlock made his way to Norman, Oklahoma, where, as an assistant, he helped guide the Sooners to the College World Series in 2010.

Meanwhile, Texas Tech was struggling, which is why Tadlock's comments about Omaha at his introductory press conference in 2012 seemed so audacious at the time. After all, he was inheriting a team that had just finished dead last in Big 12 play. But with trips to the College World Series in 2014, 2016, 2018, and 2019, as well as conference championships in 2016, 2017, and 2019, and a No. 1 ranking during the COVID-shortened 2020 season, Omaha was no longer just a goal, but an expectation.

Make no mistake: Larry Hays laid the foundation for Texas Tech baseball, but Tim Tadlock carried it to the next level. Fans entering Dan Law Field at Rip Griffin Park enjoy one of the best atmospheres in all of college baseball and give Red Raider players one of the best home-field advantages in the country.

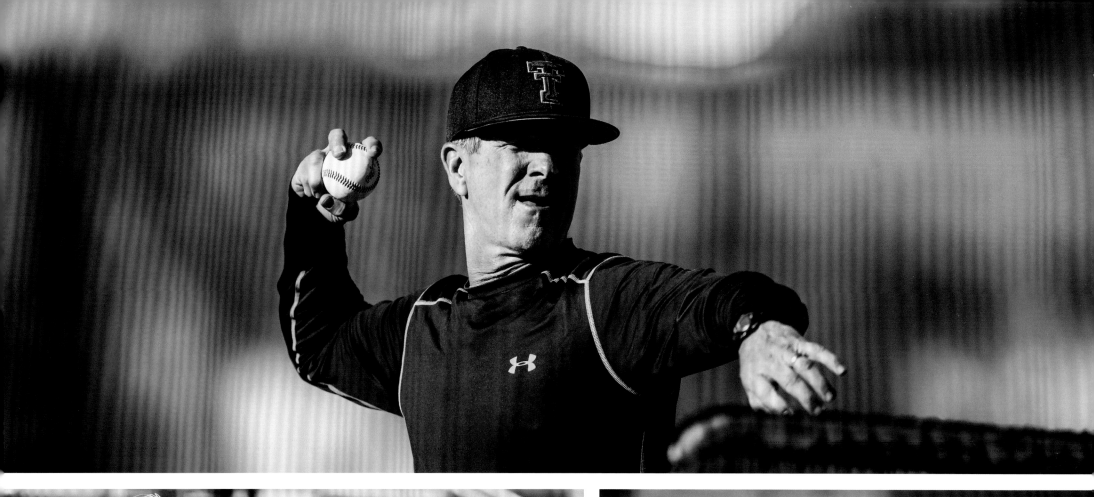

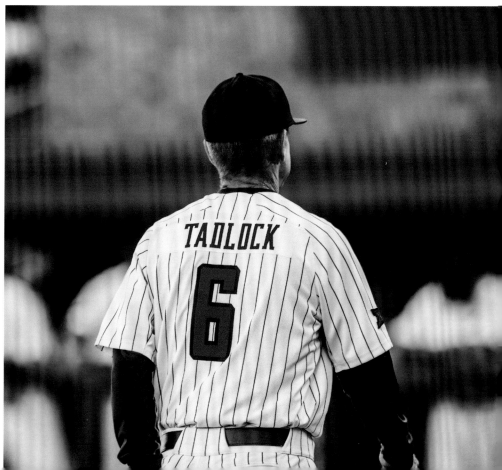

Elmer Tarbox

Elmer Tarbox

Born in 1916 near Bishop, Oklahoma Territory, Elmer Tarbox grew up in tiny Higgins, Texas, during the Depression. He worked at various jobs to help the family make ends meet and stood out in athletics and academics. Tarbox lettered four years in basketball, excelled in track, became an Eagle Scout, joined the Citizens Military Training Camp at Fort Sill, Oklahoma, during the summers, and graduated valedictorian of his high school class in 1935.

He came to Texas Technological College seeking an athletic scholarship and, with raw talent and hard work, created a national reputation for himself. He lettered two years in football, three years in basketball, and three years in track, where he served as team captain in 1938. He won the high and low hurdles Border Conference competition and the West Texas AAU Light Heavyweight Championship the same year. In football, he became seventh in the nation in rushing and receiving, tied for tenth nationally in passes received, and led the nation in interceptions with eleven. Pop Warner named Tarbox to his 1938 All-American Team and he became the "Wheaties Cereal Champion." In 1939, among other honors, Tarbox was named outstanding player at the Cotton Bowl. He served as president of his sophomore and junior classes, graduated with a B average in business administration, and was listed in Marquis' *Who's Who in the South*. The NFL named him the 18th pick in the nation in the 1939 draft, but by 1940 he became a pilot trainee in the US Army Air Corps in advance of America's entry into World War II.

As a B-25 pilot, Tarbox served in the China, Burma, and India theater of operations as one of General Clare Chennault's Flying Tiger bomber pilots, flying the "Hump" between India and China, bombing strategic targets. After being wounded, Tarbox took over armament and bomb site maintenance for the entire theater. He developed the "wobble gun" that remedied a blind spot on B-25s, saving untold lives, and developed improved landing pattern and traffic controls and air-sea rescue operations. He received the Silver Star for gallantry, the Purple Heart, and the Air Medal, among other awards.

After the war, Tarbox married his high school sweetheart, raised a family, and found business success with Elmer's Weights, which increased performance for athletes. Coach Pete Cawthon put Tarbox in touch with the president of Sears, Roebuck & Co. stores, which sold his weights, as later did 1,600 Kmart stores. Tarbox also served five terms as representative of the 76th District of Texas in the legislature and, with Governor Preston Smith, helped create the Tech medical school and provided strong support for Tech's fledgling law school. Unfortunately, Parkinson's disease afflicted him by 1968, leading Tarbox to establish a Parkinson's Disease Institute at Tech, which he supported until his death in 1987.

Coach Cawthon called Tarbox "Elmer the Great!" He became a Distinguished Alumnus of Tech, and in 2021 his name was added to the Ring of Honor at Jones AT&T Stadium, a fitting tribute to a conspicuous alumnus who, despite adversity, served his school, state, and country with honor.

Image courtesy of the Southwest Collection / Special Collections Library

LIVING

TEXAS TECH

Angela Braly

Angela Braly strode through open doors on her way to running a massive health-care company and being named the fourth most powerful woman in the world by *Forbes* magazine in 2008. Now she's passionate about keeping doors open for other women.

Braly grew up in the Dallas–Fort Worth metroplex suburb of Richardson, where she was on the high school drill team—"a very Texas thing to do," she said. She followed her sister to Texas Tech and got a degree in business and finance, where she felt supported and encouraged. Braly was born toward the end of the Baby Boomer generation and didn't encounter the sexism some women a few years older had faced. There were many other women already studying business when she came to Lubbock. One of her roommates ended up in pharmaceutical sales and another went into the business side of the fashion industry.

Braly enjoyed herself: football games, visiting Buddy Holly's gravesite and Prairie Dog Town, going to a drive-in for milkshakes with Snickers bars in them, and making life-long "fun friends."

"There was such an effortless sense of community at Texas Tech, it was easy to get involved," she said. Braly was a Tri Delt, involved in student government, and had a job handing out equipment at a gym where she had lots of time to do homework. Working within organizations, she developed both leadership and saving skills. On Sundays the dorms didn't serve food, and Braly would use coupons to get an almost-free burrito—her total cost was the 17-cent sales tax.

As for her formal education, Braly finished in three years.

"I was in a hurry," she said, adding that she doesn't advise other students to follow her example. Law school at SMU followed because, as she put it, "A lot of reasons things happen in business was because of the law." Braly started working for a law firm and helping a health-care client.

"The personal story was very compelling to me, and it was a real attraction," Braly related. She moved into the health-care industry and eventually became president and CEO of WellPoint (now Anthem), the nation's largest health insurer in terms of members, representing 34 million people, or one in nine Americans. She became WellPoint's board chair in 2010.

Braly left the company in 2012 and founded The Braly Group. She works as a consultant and speaker and acts on behalf of philanthropic enterprises. Braly also serves on the board of directors for The Procter & Gamble Company, Lowe's Companies, ExxonMobil, and Brookfield Asset Management, where she utilizes her leadership and expertise in corporate governance. Her particular emphasis is remedying the lack of women on corporate boards. She has been honored by Direct Women, an organization working to get women in law on corporate boards.

"If I could be CEO of a Fortune 50 company and on boards, I thought lots of women would and it hasn't happened," she said. Part of her effort in that direction was starting The Policy Circle to encourage more women to be involved in public policy.

"We found women were mostly involved in politics or women's issues—but not general public policy," she said. The organization is now in forty-six states and four countries. Women get together, like members of a book club, but instead of reading a book they read a brief on public policy issues like economics, health care, immigration, and education. The women are then encouraged to get involved in their communities.

"I feel it's part of my responsibility to help women find their way along that path," Braly said.

Image courtesy of the Rawls College of Business

"There was such an effortless sense of community at Texas Tech, it was easy to get involved."

Charles Q. Brown Jr.

Two former Red Raiders made *Time* magazine's list of the 100 most influential people for 2020. One is the quarterback for the Kansas City Chiefs. The other flies planes and is the first African American to lead a US military service: the Chief of Staff of the United States Air Force, General Charles Q. Brown Jr.

General Charles Q. Brown Jr., known as C. Q., is the commander of the Pacific Air Forces, air component commander of the US Indo-Pacific Command, and the executive director of the Pacific Air Combat Operations Staff at Joint Base Pearl Harbor. Unanimously confirmed by the US Senate, General Brown is the first Black officer to sit on the Joint Chiefs of Staff since General Colin Powell served as chair. General Brown has earned the Legion of Merit with three oak clusters, the Defense Distinguished Service Medal with one bronze oak leaf cluster, the Air Force Distinguished Service Medal, the Defense Superior Service Medal, and the Bronze Star, among many other awards.

General Brown served in numerous positions, including as aide-de-camp to the Chief of Staff of the Air Force, director of the Secretary of the Air Force, and Chief of Staff Executive Action Group and deputy director of the Operations Directorate in the US Central Command. He was a National Defense Fellow at the Institute for Defense Analyses and has commanded a fighter squadron, the US Air Force Weapons School, two fighter wings, and US Air Forces Central Command. He served as the Deputy Commander, US Central Command.

As Chief of Staff of the US Air Force, General Brown sits as a member of the Joint Chiefs of Staff and represents the Air Force to the United States citizenry, industry partners, and diplomatic allies. He strategizes and communicates Air Force priorities and shapes its culture, vision, and operations while managing the organization and training of 685,000 active-duty, Guard, Reserve, and civilian personnel. He is central to integrating warfighting operations including intelligence across all domains—air, sea, land, cyber, and space— throughout all the military branches.

General Brown earned his degree from Texas Tech in 1984 with a major in civil engineering and was commissioned as a distinguished graduate of the ROTC program. He credits his love of flying to Texas Tech and the opportunities afforded him at the university. When he first arrived at TTU, he had planned to get his degree and become an engineer. He intended to complete his four years in the Air Force and get out, but his experience with the ROTC at Texas Tech changed his mind. He wanted to be a pilot. Acting as cadet corps commander the first semester of his senior year sealed the deal. He was going to fly fighter jets, and he was going to be a difference maker. He just wouldn't realize the extent of the difference he would make—as someone who serves his country, who inspires young people, who protects our nation, who is blazing trails, breaking barriers, and breathing excellence into his work as a leader, teacher, mentor, and guide.

Images courtesy of the United States Air Force

Brown's 1986 Pilot Training Graduation

Brown speaking on Veterans Day in New York City

Brown receiving Red Jacket as Tuskegee Airman

Brown speaking at AFA Symposium

Barry Corbin

Leonard Barrie Corbin was perhaps always destined for a career in the theatrical arts. His mother, Alma LaMerle Scott, an elementary teacher, named her first-born after Scottish novelist and playwright James Matthew Barrie, author of the children's classic *Peter Pan*. Siblings Blaine and Jane followed. Blaine Corbin Sr., their father, was a Lubbock attorney and two-term Texas Senate Democratic member, the youngest at the time, who was succeeded by Preston Smith.

At age seven, Barry Corbin knew he wanted to be an actor. While his friends envisioned growing up to be cowboys or astronauts, Corbin auditioned for roles on the stage and took dancing lessons. Initial shyness at performing in front of others was overcome by visualizing the live audience as just another character within the production. At Monterey High School, he joined Future Farmers of American and gave a brief try at playing football, but it was theater that drew his attention.

He enrolled as a theatre major in 1959 at Texas Tech University, his father's alma mater. A two-year stint in the US Marine Corps briefly diverted his focus on college. Returning to Tech, Corbin struck up a friendship with G. W. Bailey, four years his junior, and persuaded Bailey to become an actor. The duo were castmates in 1964 productions of *The Firebugs* and *Romeo and Juliet*. Years later, when Corbin began writing scripts and radio plays, Bailey played opposite Corbin in a skit about two cowboys waiting on the side of a road for a buddy. They reunited in Lubbock in April 1982 to play gravediggers in Texas Tech's production of *Hamlet*, then were named adjunct professors of theatre arts at Tech and were inducted into the West Texas Walk of Fame in 1985. The pair also played opposite one another in TV episodes of *The Closer* from 2007 to 2012.

The ability to memorize large volumes of dialogue and immerse himself into a variety of characters has enabled Corbin to fluidly crosswalk between the mediums of theater, television, and film in a career spanning more than four decades. Corbin has embodied a number of Shakespearean characters on the stage throughout the United States. His most prominent roles on the big and small screen include *Urban Cowboy*, *The Thorn Birds*, *WarGames*, *Dallas*, *Lonesome Dove*, *No Country for Old Men*, and *Northern Exposure*, for which he earned an Emmy nomination.

Portraying a cowboy, though, resonates closest to home for Corbin. It's a part he's embraced fully, from living and running his own ranch to raising cattle and buffalo and riding horses. Westerns are his favorite genre of film and book. His deep, booming voice, with its distinct Texan accent, comes in handy when portraying characters such as the legendary rancher Charles Goodnight, narrating documentaries and audiobooks, and voicing promos for Fort Worth country-music station 99.5 The Wolf for more than two decades. In 1992, the National Cowboy Hall of Fame honored Corbin with the Western Heritage "Wrangler" Award for his role in the TV-movie adaptation of Louis L'Amour's *Conagher*.

Left: Corbin in a TTU production of The Merry Wives of Windsor.
Bottom right: Corbin (right) and Durwood Jacobs in a Texas Tech production of Five Finger Exercise *that ran January 25–31, 1962.*
Images courtesy of the Southwest Collection / Special Collections Library

At age seven, Barry Corbin knew he wanted to be an actor.

Stella Ruth Crockett Courtney

Born on October 4, 1943, in Lubbock, Texas, Estella "Stella" Ruth Crockett was a member of the Dunbar High School band and one of a small number of graduating seniors in late spring 1961. Her instrument of choice, the clarinet, was her ticket to a band scholarship at Langston University, a historically black school in Langston, Oklahoma, popular with Lubbock African American students seeking college degrees. She had visions of playing in the college band, living in a campus dormitory, and socializing with others of her own age hailing from a variety of cities other than her hometown. It was to be her first time living away from home.

All those plans went out the window following the July 17 announcement by Mayor David Casey, on behalf of the Texas Tech Board of Directors, that the university would accept applications from Black students starting with the fall semester. Elated at the news Texas Tech would finally integrate, Dunbar's band director, Roy Roberts, reached out to his recent graduates in an effort to convince them to enroll. Stella accepted that challenge, joining a very small group of Black students who decided to attend. They formed a support system for each other. Although her hopes to live in a campus dorm didn't materialize, Stella was able to continue her musical training by joining the Texas Tech marching band, then led by Dean Killion.

Being the first to break the long-held race barrier at the university was no easy task. The new students faced discrimination inside the classroom, around campus, and on out-of-town band trips. Stella had to enroll in another section of a psychology course because the first instructor publicly used disparaging language toward her. Encouragement from her family, church, and community helped Stella stay on course.

She credits her mother's advice for "sticking it out" as a prime motivator for overcoming her struggles during the four-year commitment. "It's my right to be here. I deserve an education, and I'm going to get it," she reminisced in a March 3, 2010, Southwest Collection oral history interview.

Influenced by strong mentors, Stella knew from the second grade she wanted to be an educator. Her student-teaching position at Phillis Wheatley Elementary placed her under the supervision of Hazel Scott Taylor, who may have been the first African American to earn a doctoral degree from the TTU College of Education and whom Stella cites as the motivator for her choosing to concentrate in special education.

In May 1965, Stella earned her bachelor's degree in elementary education, thereby becoming the first African American to attend Lubbock schools from K–12, attend all undergraduate years at Texas Tech, and successfully graduate. She turned down a job offer from the Lubbock Independent School District to teach in New Mexico, then attended Michigan State University to earn a master's degree in special education and taught disabled adults in Rhode Island. Stella married Delton Courtney, a union that lasted more than fifty years, and had three children. Retired in June 2009 after forty-three years of teaching, she continued to stay involved in education through her church's Sunday school program and membership in the American Federation of Teachers.

"It's my right to be here. I deserve an education, and I'm going to get it."

Jack Dale

Dub Malaise was one of the greatest basketball players in Texas Tech history, and the reason Malaise wanted to become a Red Raider was Jack Dale.

"Dub told me, 'I used to listen to your games with Jack Dale. That's where I wanted to go to school because he made them so exciting," said Gerald Myers, former Red Raider player, head basketball coach, and athletic director. Malaise still owns the school record for most games scoring over thirty points. The assist goes to Jack Dale, sportscaster.

Dale called more than 1,500 Red Raider games for more than fifty years over a storied career. He was inducted into the Texas Sports Hall of Fame in 2005 as part of a charter group of Texas media legends such as Verne Lundquist, Frank Fallon, Dave Campbell, Dan Jenkins, and Blackie Sherrod. His time at Tech stretched from 1953 into the early years of the Bob Knight era in 2003. Even though it's been two decades since Dale retired, fans still remember his signature phrases in that distinctive baritone:

"He jumps, shoots, *and* scores!"

"In and out . . . and back in again!"

Fans watching their Red Raiders on television would turn down the sound and listen to Dale's rapid-fire radio broadcast. "There was nobody I've heard before or since who could hold a candle to Jack as far as creating a game, knowing where the ball was, who had the ball and created the excitement," said Gary Ashby, former Red Raider baseball player, who called baseball games with Dale.

Dale, a native Kansan, grew up calling imaginary games on his family's farm. He was trained as a sportscaster in the early 1950s to be a reporter and not favor one team over the other. He never called the Red Raiders "we" or "us." "He was a professional's professional," said Myers. Part of that function was doing a sportscaster's homework. In one instance, the Red Raiders were playing an exhibition against a Yugoslavian team. Dale went over the names until he could pronounce them flawlessly—and did so during the game.

That professionalism led to respect. When former Red Raider hoops coach Bob Bass became head coach of the San Antonio Spurs when they were in the old American Basketball Association, he asked Dale to become the voice of the Spurs for more money. Dale turned Bass down. He liked what he did and liked living in Lubbock with his family. He was also a man of deep faith who carried a hand-sized Bible in his shirt pocket, reading it on road trips.

Over the decades, Dale made an impact across Texas. At a 2003 "roast" in Austin to honor Dale on his retirement, a number of people with connections to Texas Tech spoke. But one other person stopped by to thank Dale for his iconic career: legendary Texas football coach Darrell Royal. Dale also pioneered a sports talk radio show in Lubbock on KFYO with his son Steve in 1992 and continued to do it after retiring from play-by-play work. He was surprisingly introverted and quiet away from the microphone—but that didn't get in the way of another part of his job, selling KFYO radio advertising.

The death of his wife Sue in early 2011 hit Dale hard, and he passed away in July of that year. Ten years later, his son Steve passed away after a successful sportscasting career.

The people who remember Jack Dale as a great sportscaster also call him an equally great person.

"He was one of my favorite people of all time," said Myers.

Images courtesy of Texas Tech Athletics

Abner Euresti and Karin McCay

When local Lubbock kid Abner Euresti graduated from Texas Tech University, the school down the road, he did not imagine that he would be the truthteller of the community for multiple generations of Lubbockites. When Karin McCay earned her degree from Texas Tech, she did not imagine that she would be the truthteller of the community for multiple generations of Lubbockites. And neither Abner nor Karin imagined that they would be doing it together. Karin and Abner are those rare partners in media, the ones who find their homes in the communities where they find their hearts. And although they would have many opportunities to move beyond the Lubbock market, to work from small to medium to large market newsrooms, they knew they not only had a good thing; they had a calling in the South Plains. Together, they anchored the KCBD evening news for more than thirty years and have the privilege and the pleasure of being the longest-running anchor team in the United States.

And yes, they were wooed by other stations. They won enough awards and earned enough accolades to turn numerous heads. Karin is a 17-time winner of the Anson Jones Award selected by the Texas Medical Association for her outstanding work as a health reporter. She was given the prestigious Edward R. Murrow Award three times and won an Emmy Award for her documentary on the first South Plains Honors Flight. Abner has been recognized by the Texas State Teachers Association, the Association of Texas Professional Educators, the Texas Parent Teacher Association, and the Texas Associated Press Broadcasters Division. Abner was praised for his advocacy of educational equity, access, and opportunity, especially for at-risk students, with a State Board of Education Hero Award. They have also won joint awards—the Lubbock Area Foundation Hero's Award and the Children's Miracle Network Lifetime Achievement Award. As cohosts of the Children's Miracle Network Telethon since 1984, Abner and Karin have helped raise more than $17 million for the Children's Hospital at the University Medical Center.

Both have been witnesses to history and influencers in their community. Abner reported on the desegregation of Lubbock schools—having himself been subjected to and a graduate of the segregated school system. Abner was there when a federal judge ruled that the old Lubbock County Jail was unconstitutional. Karin wrote some of the most powerful pieces to come out of the South Plains. Her first medical story, "Minor Moms," a five-part series on the epidemic of young mothers in Lubbock, won her first award. Her piece, "Trying or Dying to Quit," that followed nine teenagers who attempted to stop smoking for one month, continues to be on a national list of films recommended to public schools.

When Abner returned to Texas Tech in December 2017 to serve as the speaker for the commencement exercises, he paid tribute to his alma mater. And he honored his best friend and television partner, Karin, because, over those past forty years, she had been his best friend and partner-on-air. Karin believed in him and proudly shared the desk with him. As she explains, "In the beginning, there was so much prejudice. People called and wanted him off the air because of the color of his skin. I was horrified. . . . I couldn't believe it. He was so hurt, but he kept going and he was strong. . . . [H]e had the heart and the drive to keep on going." As our truthtellers, Karin and Abner have been central to shaping how we understand our histories, our culture, and the shape of the changes yet to come.

Image courtesy of the Southwest Collection / Special Collections Library

Maxine Fry

Maxine Fry was born in Lockney, Texas, on July 5, 1917, to Robert Ernest and Ruby Britton Fry, early settlers of Floyd County. Graduating from Floydada High School at the age of seventeen, Maxine entered Texas Technological College in 1934 as a freshman during a time when women made up 40 percent of the total 2,328 undergraduate student body and more than 53 percent of the graduate student body. Maxine was among the first wave of female students to live in Women's Dormitory No. 1, renamed Doak Hall in 1952. She occupied the same dorm room for the four years she attended Texas Tech, two of which were shared with her younger sister, Marilynn. Both were very active in campus activities and leadership roles, earning them the affectionate moniker "the Fry sisters from Floydada."

Strikingly beautiful and outgoing, Maxine selected journalism as a major and occasionally served as a reporter for the campus newspaper, *The Toreador*. She was inducted into The Forum, later renamed Mortar Board, and served as president of Las Chaparritas, a local sorority that become Kappa Kappa Gamma. She won several school beauty contests and was chosen as the 1938 Sun Bowl Princess. In 1936, she was encouraged to run for student council president, a role that was primarily male dominated throughout the state. With the support of Marilynn and friends, who banded together to enthusiastically campaign on her behalf, Maxine became the first elected female president of the student council in May 1937, a milestone not reached at UT nor Texas A&M until 1975 and 1994 respectively.

Assisted by classmate and close pal Arch Lamb and his newly formed all-male booster organization, the Saddle Tramps, Maxine was able to successfully reinstate the school's bonfire tradition after it had been banned by school administrators following outrage by Lubbock citizens over vandalism and theft of wood by Texas Tech students. Her administration also wrote a revision of the student council's constitution.

Following graduation in 1938, Maxine taught journalism for two years in Littlefield and Grandfalls, worked on *The Midlander* magazine its first seven years in publication, and was a charter member of the Midland Symphony Guild. She wed Hugh McCullough, who served as her vice-president on student council, in 1940. They transferred to Midland in 1941 for his job with The Texas Company, later Sinclair Oil and Gas Company, then relocated in 1942 when Hugh became a special agent for the Federal Bureau of Investigation. Upon returning to Midland in 1950, Hugh worked as an independent geologist. During the course of their fifty years of marriage, the couple had three children: Robert Fry, Linda, and Mary Kay. The McCulloughs were charter members of St. Luke's United Methodist Church in Midland, where Maxine held a variety of positions including serving as president of the United Methodist Women. They managed to visit all fifty states prior to Hugh's passing in 1991. Maxine passed away on March 21, 2012, in El Paso, Texas, at the age of 94.

Joe Kirk Fulton

Texas Tech Masked Rider Corey Waggoner brought his horse Fearless Champion to Joe Kirk Fulton's 2013 funeral. Boots were sideways and backwards in the stirrups to honor the horseman who created the university's iconic mascot. Fulton was the first official Masked Rider in 1954, but not the first masked rider atop a horse on campus. In 1936, George Tate wore a mask and scarlet cape on a palomino named Tony before a football game against TCU and its star quarterback Sammy Baugh. Tate made a few more appearances—the Ghost Rider—but that was it.

Almost two decades later, Texas Tech was trying to get into the Southwest Conference. All SWC teams had a mascot. Fulton's son Tim said his dad rode a horse into the student union while masked during rodeo week as a prank. Football coach DeWitt Weaver approached Fulton and asked if he'd lead the Red Raiders onto the field. Fulton said yes, had chaps made in Fort Worth, and created an all-black outfit. Fulton—who'd grown up riding his pony Shorty as a kid—didn't have a black horse, though. He borrowed Blackie from the Hockley County Sheriff's Posse and made his debut at the Gator Bowl in Jacksonville on January 1, 1954, where Tech beat Auburn 35–13.

"No team in any bowl game made a more sensational entrance," wrote Ed Danforth of the *Atlanta Journal*.

Gerald Myers, athletics director emeritus, said, "I don't think anybody realized when he made that ride in 1954 how important of a tradition the Masked Rider and horse would become for Texas Tech." Jim Cloyd took the reins for the 1955–56 year and more than sixty Masked Riders have followed.

The Associated Press ranked the Masked Rider the ninth-best mascot in college football in 2010, and Texas Tech's football game entrance has consistently ranked in many top-ten lists with the Masked Rider as the centerpiece. Fulton served as Masked Rider for the 1954–55 school year. During a game against LSU, Fulton was going around the entire stadium—as was the practice back then—and got tangled up with LSU's head cheerleader, who was not seriously injured. The next day Weaver told Fulton, "I don't care how many cheerleaders you run over. Just make sure you get the quarterback first."

After Fulton left Tech he got into his family's businesses—ranching, banking, oil and gas, land development and investments. The Texas Tech legend also became a legend in the world of horses. Fulton was fascinated by genetics and worked on breeding equine perfection. Fulton mostly bred cutting horses and quarter horses—a business his family still runs.

He entered the American Quarter Horse Association Hall of Fame two years before he died. Horses he bred won more than $16 million on the racetrack and sired winners of more than $60 million.

Fulton followed Tech sports and rarely missed a football game. And he still got chills when the Masked Rider sprinted down the Jones AT&T Stadium field. "He loved the tradition it became. He never thought it was going to be as big as it was and he was glad," said his son.

Tim Fulton runs into people who wonder if he's related to the first Masked Rider. Sometimes the connection helps. He was pulled over outside of Brady and showed his license. The officer asked if he was from Lubbock. Tim said yes. The officer mentioned he was a Red Raider. Tim told him the story about his dad. He got off with a warning.

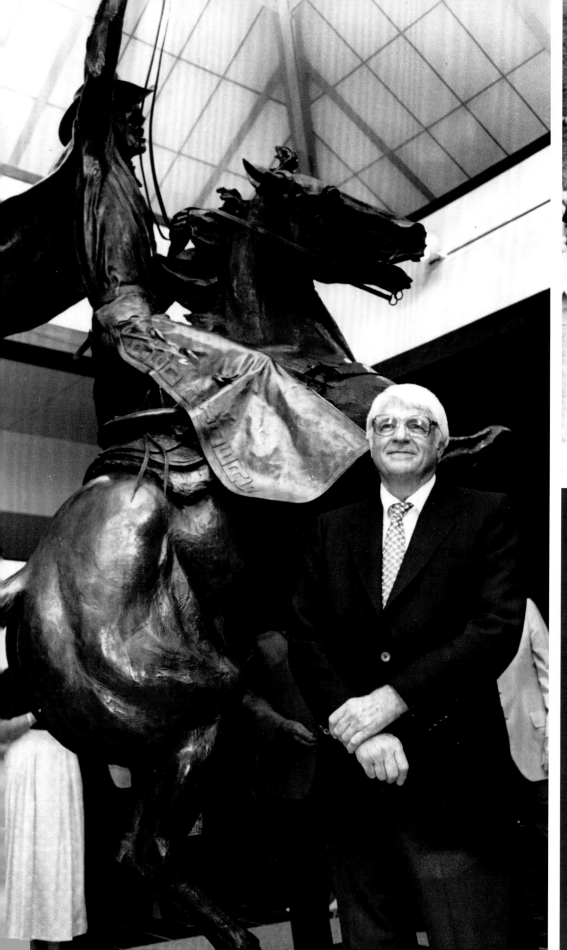

"I don't think anybody realized when he made that ride in 1954 how important of a tradition the Masked Rider and horse would become for Texas Tech."

Glenna Goodacre

For Glenna Goodacre, art was not a choice but a calling. And perhaps that is why, despite those who doubted her abilities, she continued her craft. Because she was not creating for them, she was creating for those who were not always seen, not always heard, not always recognized. In her sculptures, she rendered her subjects not only visible but present. In her work, she called into life not only people but souls. In her art, she saw not only the beauty but the lines, the bruises, the grit, the resistance.

In that vein, Glenna had to push back against a society that she feared would not accept her as a woman artist. In fact, despite being one of the very few women artists creating large-scale statues commemorating some of the most important moments in our shared history, or perhaps because of it, she signed many of her early works G. Goodacre, out of apprehension that audiences would not accept or appreciate work made by a woman.

Glenna's works, sculptures and paintings, have been exhibited in galleries, museums, and collections in over forty countries and include such monumental, commemorative pieces as the Vietnam Women's Memorial on the National Mall in Washington, DC; the Irish Memorial, dedicated to the Irish Potato Famine or Great Hunger, at Penn's Landing in Philadelphia; and *After the Ride*, a statue of President Ronald Reagan at the Reagan Presidential Library in California. In 1999, after a nationwide competition for the design of the Sacagawea dollar coin, Glenna Goodacre's interpretation of the Shoshone woman guide and her young son, Jean Baptiste Charbonneau, was selected as the winning entry.

Glenna worked at the National Academy of Design and was a fellow of the National Sculpture Society. In 2002, she won the James Earl Fraser Sculpture Award at the Prix de West Exhibition and in 2003 was awarded the Texas Medal of Arts and the Gold Medal for Career Achievement from the Portrait Society of America and was inducted into the National Cowgirl Museum and Hall of Fame.

Glenna was born in Lubbock to a legacy family, the Maxeys. Both her grandfather, James, and her father, Homer, were well respected city leaders, her father graduating from Texas Tech and becoming the first president of the Red Raider Club. And even if Glenna never attended Texas Tech—choosing Colorado College and taking classes at the Art Students League in New York—Lubbock and TTU were still a part of her memory and inspiration.

In 1969, when she was back in Lubbock, a local foundry owner gave her some clay and told her to try sculpting something. Using a paring knife, a toothpick, and a bobby pin, Glenna created a small figure of her daughter, Jill. And she found her medium.

Although Glenna called Santa Fe home for many years, Lubbock houses many of her sculptures and some of the most beloved art pieces in the public art collection of Texas Tech. *Preston Smith* greets faculty, students, and staff at the entrance of the Administration Building. *Park Place*, a piece in front of the College of Human Sciences, traces the different phases of our lives as human beings. And *CEO*, a gift to the Rawls College of Business Administration—a six-foot four-inch sculpture of a powerful businesswoman in action—charges all of us in the Texas Tech community to take on the grand challenges that face us as a global community. And just as Glenna breathed life into her sculptures, her sculptures breathe life into us, fortifying us with grit and resistance to head into the next century.

Pat Green

Pat Green came to Texas Tech to create things with his imagination—maybe be an architect or engineer. He learned he could do the same with music and picked up some famous teachers who were not part of the Texas Tech faculty. Walt Wilkins—how to write songs. Jerry Jeff Walker—the music business. Willie Nelson—his big break. Green went on to make albums, chart hit songs, tour with his "teachers" and Keith Urban, Kenny Chesney, the Dave Matthews Band, and more.

Green had an electric guitar and amp as a high schooler in Waco but couldn't play it loud. Same when he was living in Tech's Coleman Hall. So he got an acoustic guitar and started learning in his dorm's basement laundromat. Green came to Tech because his stepdad and sister were Red Raiders—and one other reason. "They accepted me," he said on a Zoom call from his Fort Worth office.

Green was gigging around Lubbock by his junior year, playing at places—as he put it—meant for college bands. He played a lot of Willie and Waylon covers. He joined the FarmHouse—a Christian-based fraternity. He graduated with an English degree in 1997—seven years after coming to Lubbock. "I tell people college was the best ten years of my life," he said.

Green, ready to make his first album, was told to call Don Caldwell, who had a Lubbock recording studio. Caldwell said he needed a producer and to call Lloyd Maines, a member of the Maines Brothers Band and father of Natalie Maines, a member of the Grammy-winning Dixie Chicks who also sang on Green's albums. Green the producer at a Mexican restaurant on Avenue Q and was told it would cost $10,000 to make the album. He got the money together and put out an album. A second album followed. "They were different than what was going on in Texas music at the time—different enough to make me stand apart," he said.

Green was opening for Willie Nelson at the Library in Lubbock and told Poodie Locke—Willie's longtime stage manager—he'd do free shows at a Texas club Locke owned if he'd get Green a slot at Willie's famed Fourth of July picnic. He did the gigs for Locke and his big break came at Willie's 1998 Fourth of July event in Luckenbach. A sign of his success over the years was 2018's *Dancehall Dreamin': A Tribute to Pat Green*, an album of musicians recording his songs, including Red Raiders William Clark Green, Cory Morrow, and Josh Abbott.

"I'm close with all those guys—close with everybody who's on that record. They did that without my knowledge; I think they were just trying to point out that I'm old," said Green, who turned 50 shortly before his alma mater's centennial celebration kicked off. He was named a Texas Tech Distinguished Alumni in 2017, along with famed heart surgeon Dr. Wayne Isom, whose niece was a college roommate of Green's wife Kori. There's another honor. Green's "I Like Texas" is the Texas Rangers victory song.

Green loves his alma mater because it's real. "The people are mostly like me, came up from a rural background or a smaller-town background. It's not about being fancy, it's about being real. A place of honesty. And I met my wife there," he said. They met at a keg party at Kori's cousin's house. Green was playing guitar by a fireplace, and they've been together since. And that's where he gets his inspiration.

"Almost all my songs I've written are about one person. So it's nice," he said.

Images courtesy of Texas Tech College of Arts and Sciences

Pat Green came to Texas Tech to create things with his imagination—maybe be an architect or engineer. He learned he could do the same with music.

Holly Hunt

When Holly Hunt's parents built a house in Anson, Texas, her mom decorated it with neutral colors and walnut furniture that lasted. Hunt wanted her room painted light green with blonde furniture.

"I always wanted to be different," said Hunt, from her place in Aspen, Colorado. She *was* different—and very successful. In 2014, Hunt sold the Chicago-based luxury design company Holly Hunt for $95 million to Knoll. Inspired by Oscar-winning costume designer Edith Head—whose name she saw in credits on dates at drive-in movies—she admired the classy style of stars Audrey Hepburn and Ava Gardner.

Hunt made her own clothes. Her mother would take her a bit south to Abilene to buy textiles. "My mom would finance it and I'd make it. They looked fabulous. I liked making clothes for parties; I wanted to have a good time," she said. Hunt made her first dress in sixth grade. Over time she would use the popular McCall's patterns as a starting point and create her own finished outfits. Coco Chanel was the topic for a final paper her senior year of high school.

Hunt went 150 miles northwest to Texas Tech to get out of Anson, join some friends, and have new experiences. She wanted to be a designer but wasn't sure how. Lubbock was not the Milan of the West, but she'd figure it out. Hunt majored in English literature with a minor in history. She took a class on clothing and textiles but hoped there was more design included. She went to parties, hung out with friends, drank beer—"small-town stuff all the way," she said.

A counselor at Tech suggested a training program with Federated Department Stores and Hunt went on to get what she called her "Masters of Business Federated." She learned from the basement up—client first, customer service, quality of product and design. "It's what made me successful later,"

she said decades afterwards. Hunt met a man, married, and settled in Chicago, where they built a successful company leasing truck trailers to railroads. She fed her desire to design by decorating their homes. Then the couple divorced, and Hunt needed a job.

She learned independence and the freedom of making her own decisions at Texas Tech. Hunt bought showroom space in Chicago's Merchandise Mart. It took her three years to turn a profit, all while trying to raise her children. Her company made 20 percent selling other people's things. So she decided to make her own furniture. Her showrooms were airy and large. Always ambitious, she quickly opened several. She saw work by designer Christian Liaigre and got on a plane to France with two employees to pitch working with him. He said yes.

Her life has taken her around the world, but there's still a sense of West Texas in her work. "Scale . . . doing things on a larger scale. Bigger space, higher ceilings. Texas is large and big," she said. The girl from Anson became a legend in the design industry with a 4,600-square-foot residence on Chicago's Gold Coast overlooking Lake Michigan.

As her success grew, she told her mom she didn't feel like she was helping anyone with her nice showrooms. Her mother asked how many people she employed. Hunt said about twenty people. Her mother asked if they were supporting their families. Holly said yes. "I didn't feel guilty anymore," she said.

Images courtesy of the Texas Tech College of Arts and Sciences

Rick and Evelyn Husband

There are certain memories in our history that we share, times when we all remember exactly where we were. One of those moments was on February 1, 2003: the return of the space shuttle Columbia. It was supposed to land in Florida after its sixteen-day mission, but the shuttle broke up over Texas just sixteen minutes before its scheduled landing. There were no survivors.

Rick Husband, commander of the Columbia, worked alongside Michael Anderson (payload commander), David Brown (mission specialist), Kalpana Chawla (mission specialist), Laurel Clark (mission specialist), Ilan Ramon (payload specialist), and Willie McCool (pilot).

A Lubbockite, Rick had attended Coronado High School and had Texas Tech faculty members for parents. He entered TTU in 1975 to pursue a degree in engineering so that he could achieve his lifelong dream of becoming an astronaut. At a Red Raiders basketball game, he met a young woman named Evelyn he could not forget. She had attended Amarillo High School just as he had, and although their paths had not crossed in Amarillo, they were lovestruck in Lubbock.

And while his heart was firmly on the ground with Evelyn, his eyes were on the skies, always on the lookout for an opportunity to explore space. He wrote to NASA from Murdough Hall, asking for more information on becoming an astronaut pilot or a mission specialist. He joined the ROTC and when he graduated in 1980, he was commissioned a second lieutenant in the US Air Force. While Rick moved to Enid, Oklahoma, for pilot training, Evelyn moved to Dallas to work for WBAP radio. Even so, they knew their destinies were intertwined, and in 1982, the two got married. They moved to Florida, where Rick continued the long journey to becoming an astronaut. He eventually earned an interview with NASA but was not selected on his first application. The second time was the charm, however, and in December 1994, he received the call that he would begin astronaut training.

When Rick was named commander of the Columbia, he was beyond excited. While quarantining, he was able to spend time with Evelyn, and the two of them celebrated the culmination of this lifelong shared dream together. Rick, for his part, wanted to make sure his family knew just how much he loved them. On the morning of the launch, January 16, 2003, Rick organized for presents to be delivered to his loved ones. He made a video for his son and one for his daughter, and in each of those tapes, he made recordings of devotionals for his children. He would be with them in their faith and study even while he was in space.

Evelyn and her children were at Kennedy Space Center waiting for Rick to come home. The countdown clock kept ticking down, but when it reached zero, it just started going back up. Evelyn knew instinctively something was wrong, but then she got the news. She was in shock. Evelyn lost her husband that day. Their children lost a father. All of us lost a hero.

But even then, as someone from NASA went back to the hotel room to help the family pack up their things and deal with the aftermath of losing the most important person in their life, she remembered to ask them to find the videotapes Rick had made for their children. And though they are bittersweet to watch, they revive a little piece of him.

Ginger Kerrick Davis

The chance discovery of a library book on astronomy and astronauts was the springboard for fostering a vision of one day exploring in person the stars and planets of outer space. At the tender age of 5, Ginger Kerrick boldly informed her parents, Kenneth and Genoveva, she wanted to work at NASA when she grew up. The memory of that declaration and the unwavering support of her father, who passed away from a heart attack at age 44 when she was 11, made a lasting impact on Ginger's life.

The youngest of four children, Kerrick was born on November 28, 1969, in El Paso, Texas. Heeding her now single mother's advice to pursue athletic and academic scholarships as a means of financing a college education, Ginger excelled in both areas, graduating as high school salutatorian and being named El Paso Female Athlete of the Year. A knee injury prior to her first game on University of Texas at El Paso's women's basketball team redirected her focus full time to pursuing a career in science. She transferred to Texas Tech, a school that had an established NASA co-op program and one that her father once attended, with the help of scholarships and student employment opportunities procured by Dr. Walter Borst of the Physics Department. In 1991 and 1993 respectively, Kerrick earned a BA and MS degree in physics.

A summer internship at Johnson Space Center in 1991 was the start of Kerrick's trajectory toward fulfilling her childhood dream. Her dogged determination to gain permanent full-time employment with NASA proved successful, despite an initial hiring freeze and later disqualification from the astronaut interview process due to a health issue. Kerrick has held multiple positions at NASA, most significantly being selected as the first non-astronaut capsule communicator in 2001 and as a flight director in 2005, making her the first Hispanic female to hold that position.

Currently Flight Integration Division Chief for NASA at Johnson Space Center, Kerrick has earned numerous accolades for her work and outreach efforts in encouraging women and students of disadvantaged backgrounds to follow their dream of a career in science. Setbacks, she often likes to say, can be overcome through hard work and sheer determination.

Earning the 2011 Women on the Move award from Texas Executive Women and being inducted into the Texas Women's Hall of Fame in the area of STEM in 2016 are among the many accomplishments Kerrick has achieved during her three decades with NASA. Through her many speaking and teaching engagements she serves as an outstanding inspiration to others seeking a career in space exploration and science. Kerrick continues a long association with her alma mater through such ventures as teaching in the STEM-MBA program in the Rawls College of Business, being a guest speaker in Kent Hance's senior seminar course, and serving as December 2010 commencement speaker. She married Samuel Davis in 2021. She was appointed to the Texas Tech Board of Regents by Governor Greg Abbott in 2019; her term expires on January 31, 2025.

Images courtesy of the Texas Tech Board of Regents

Davis alongside Chancellor Kent Hance

Anne Lynch

Anne Lynch moved back to her tiny hometown of Dell City, Texas, in 2011, a little burg just west of the Guadalupe Mountains and 90 miles east of El Paso. She had left in 1970 to go to Texas Tech for an agriculture education and it set up her business career. When Lynch got on a bus to head to Lubbock more than fifty years ago, she had no idea she'd make history as the first woman to represent Texas Tech as the Masked Rider.

It started at a football game her freshman year. It was exciting. The Goin' Band from Raiderland's music. A full—and loud—stadium with almost everybody in school colors. Then Lynch saw Masked Rider Tommy Martin take off on Charcoal Cody. She wanted to do that, too. Lynch grew up riding horses all over the Dell Valley to visit friends or travel the five miles into town. But she didn't know if the Masked Rider was a student.

During Lynch's sophomore year she learned that, first, the Masked Rider had to be a junior or senior and second, he had to be a man. A year later, Lynch returned to see about signing up to be the Masked Rider and was again told it was just for guys. She persisted. She talked to her dean. She went to a Board of Regents meeting. Eventually Lynch got an answer: "We need to look into that."

Lynch made progress independently toward her goal. She worked in the horse barn and rode the horse Happy V, who replaced Charcoal Cody. In December 1973, she was asked to try out by riding a Western Pleasure Pattern, which was easy. A month later, Lynch was told she'd be the next Masked Rider.

It was controversial. Women's rights were a hot topic. The famous Battle of the Sexes tennis match between Billie Jean King and Bobby Riggs took place in 1973. The National Organization of Women was founded less than a decade before Lynch started pursuing her Masked Rider quest.

Dirk West, who drew Texas Tech sports cartoons in the *Lubbock Avalanche-Journal*, penned one showing a woman on the horse with blonde curls, riding sidesaddle and applying lipstick. No matter that Lynch had long, straight dark hair. It was signed "Dirk West, male chauvinist pig."

She had strong backing from students, faculty, and others. "No girl was against it," said Lynch, who was also supported by the Saddle Tramps. She was a bit nervous before riding in her first football game, against Iowa State. If it wasn't perfect, she feared, it would bolster people's arguments against her. As the Goin' Band began to play the fanfare, Happy V started a sideways dance. He knew what to do, and Lynch felt it made that first ride easier. And the cheers told her she'd fought the right battle. She had a great year as the Masked Rider, even sleeping near Happy V's stable nights before games to make sure everything went well.

After graduating, Lynch went into business and married. She had four kids and spent twenty years living in Costa Rica, which is where her children were raised. Lynch got involved with the horse world in the Central American country, riding dressage. "It was a whole other universe," she said, riding as much as she could in between her children's activities.

When the Masked Rider statue was unveiled behind the Frazier Alumni Center, Lynch was there. One of the fathers of another former female Masked Rider approached her and thanked her for breaking the barrier so that his daughter and other daughters could follow.

When Lynch got on a bus to head to Lubbock more than fifty years ago, she had no idea she'd make history as the first woman to represent Texas Tech as the Masked Rider.

Welcome ANNE LYNCH

George O'Brien

Decades after becoming the only Texas Tech alum to be given the Congressional Medal of Honor, George O'Brien recorded a video and talked about what he did in Korea. "This medal is not mine," said a clearly emotional white-haired O'Brien, who died in 2005. "It belongs to those kids who never grew up to be grandfathers. I just hold it in trust and hope I wear it well, I pray."

O'Brien was born in Fort Worth and graduated from Big Spring High School. He was a seaman in the Merchant Marines around the end of World War II before coming to Texas Tech, where he received a bachelor's degree in geology. While at Tech, he enlisted as a private in the Marine Corps. After graduation, O'Brien entered Officer Candidates School. He eventually went to Korea. In late October 1952, Second Lieutenant O'Brien led Marines to overtake a strategic hill that communist forces captured the day before. It was chilly before the attack, and O'Brien sought coffee for his men. Trucks came through but instead of bringing coffee, they distributed hand grenades and gave O'Brien's Marines a ride. After walking further toward their objective, the Marines attacked. From O'Brien's Medal of Honor Citation:

Second Lieutenant O'Brien leaped from his trench when the attack signal was given and, shouting for his men to follow raced across an exposed saddle and up the enemy-held hill through a virtual hail of deadly small-arms, artillery and weapon fire. Although shot through the arm and thrown to the ground by hostile automatic-weapons fire as he neared the well-entrenched enemy position, he bravely regained his feet, waved his men onward and continued to spearhead the assault, pausing only long enough to go to the aid of a wounded Marine. Encountering the enemy at close range, he proceeded to hurl hand grenades into the bunkers and, utilizing his carbine to best advantage in savage hand-to-hand combat, succeeded in killing at least three of the enemy. Struck down by the concussion of grenades on three occasions during the subsequent action, he steadfastly refused to be evacuated for medical treatment and continued to lead his platoon in the assault for a period of nearly four hours, repeatedly encouraging his men and maintaining superb direction of the unit.

Afterwards, he set up defense for a counterattack, helping the wounded and ignoring his own wounds. He was treated on a hospital ship, returned to combat a few weeks later, and earned a second Purple Heart for additional wounds. He earned other medals from his time in Korea.

He was on a ship heading into San Francisco when told he'd receive the nation's top military honor. A year to the day after that deadly battle in Korea, President Dwight Eisenhower put the medal around O'Brien's neck in Washington, DC. O'Brien returned to West Texas and worked as a petroleum geologist. He was promoted to major in the Marine Corps Reserve.

O'Brien was tough, but fair, raising his family. "He was exactly like a Marine," said his son Robb. "We would go to restaurants and held the door for my sister and my mother and their chairs. If we didn't do it right, we'd go out and come back in and do it again." At Texas Tech, there's a scholarship in O'Brien's name for Marines and their children. After his death, he was buried in the Texas State Cemetery in Austin. Seven years later, Senator John Cornyn praised O'Brien at a ceremony renaming the Veterans Administration medical center in Big Spring the George H. O'Brien VA Medical Center. A statue in his honor stands in front of the facility.

Image courtesy of Texas Tech Communications and Marketing

George O'Brien is the only Texas Tech alum to be given the Congressional Medal of Honor.

Scott Pelley

Millions of Americans hear the voice of Scott Pelley, see the integrity in his eyes, listen to him ask the hard questions, and know instinctively that they can trust him, that he will get to the heart of the truth. And after his nearly twenty years on *60 Minutes*, we count on Scott Pelley to be the narrator of our histories, our challenges, our victories. He is one of the most experienced, most well-respected broadcast journalists in the world.

Pelley was born in San Antonio, Texas, but grew up in Lubbock and at the age of fifteen already knew he would be a journalist. The boy who would grow up to be the man who speaks for our nation started as a copyboy for the *Lubbock Avalanche-Journal*, but he was soon recognized for his talents as a writer. He found excitement and hope in the newspaper office. He understood that the media represented the Fourth Estate as a bastion to protect that most fragile and powerful of institutions, democracy. And he took that responsibility seriously.

Pelley would go on to attend Texas Tech, majoring in journalism, but even as a student, he began work as a broadcast journalist. And soon Fort Worth and Dallas came calling. But his "overnight success" was not so overnight, nor was it achieved without hard work, determination, and some courage. He became a correspondent for CBS in New York City after several years of being in the field and building a relationship with his interviewees who trusted him to tell their stories and his viewers who believed in him to tell those tales with integrity. Because Pelley lives what he teaches, he learns what he has experienced. And at the heart of his success is *writing*. "It's such an elementary thing, but something so few people get right," he has said. "It's not enough to have the story; you have to be able to tell the story." And Pelley is the master of storytelling. With style. With eloquence. With fluidity. With effortlessness. And behind that effortlessness is an enormous amount of effort. Writing. Rewriting. Rewriting again and again.

It is because of his relentless pursuit of not just the story but the right words to tell that story that has made Pelley an award-winning journalist. His stories for *60 Minutes* have accounted for half of all the major awards the show has won since he joined the program. He has won more than forty awards for his field work. He has received eight Edward R. Murrow Awards, three George Foster Peabody Awards, four Alfred I. duPont–Columbia University Award silver batons, a George Polk Award, and recognitions from the Society of Professional Journalists, the Overseas Press Club of America, Investigative Reporters and Editors, and the Writers Guild of America. Perhaps most significantly, he has been awarded Paul White Award, the highest honor from the Radio Television Digital News Association.

The impact and influence of Scott Pelley is enduring. *The Washington Times* wrote, "The legacy of Edward R. Murrow lives at CBS in the daring, long-range investigations of Scott Pelley." And Salon.com said, "He restores a little of our faith in TV news while performing hugely important, world-bettering reports along the way." As recounted in his memoir, *Truth Worth Telling: A Reporter's Search for Meaning in the Stories of Our Times*, he asked penetrating questions of dictators; exposed devastating realities of natural disasters, mass shootings, terrorism, war, famine, genocide; and celebrated the courage-defying work of first responders and those who rescued people from the rubble of war-torn countries. That is what journalists do.

Image courtesy of Texas Tech Alumni Association

After his nearly twenty years on *60 Minutes*, we count on Scott Pelley to be the narrator of our histories, our challenges, our victories.

Brenda Peters

Brenda Peters knows discrimination. She attended a segregated high school in Dallas more than a decade after segregation was ruled unconstitutional in 1954 by the US Supreme Court's *Brown v. Board of Education* decision. Her school was closed after her junior year, her school district integrated, and Peters spent her senior year at mostly white Lake Highlands High School.

After graduating with an accounting degree from Texas Tech, she landed a job in the Atlanta office of one of the Big Eight accounting firms, where she was told some clients did not want women or African Americans to work on their accounts.

In between high school and that first job, Peters met Herschel Mann, a Texas Tech accounting professor from the Deep South. Mann grew up in Arkansas, raised by parents who taught him to respect all people. He almost got in a fight once because he was rooting for the Brooklyn Dodgers—the team that integrated baseball in 1947 with Jackie Robinson. He was attending the University of Alabama in 1965 when Dr. Martin Luther King Jr. led the historic Selma to Montgomery march. Brenda Peters knew of Mann as "the student's professor," because Mann would personally invest in the success of his students, in accounting *and* life.

Peters was one of his best students, highly recruited from the moment she graduated. Texas Tech took students on field trips to visit some of the Big Eight (now Big Four) accounting firms, created an Accounting Advisory Council, and set up internship programs that almost always led to employment. Mann said the firms admired the work ethic shown by Red Raiders, even if the cost to recruit them was high. One firm calculated that by the time partners came out to Lubbock, got hotel rooms, and took a huge group to dinner at Las Brisas or the Double Nickel, the cost of recruiting Texas Tech students was the highest in the nation. But Tech students were also loyal and stayed with firms—many becoming partners. At that point, the cost of recruiting a partner was much lower.

When Brenda Peters was ready for that first job, she came to Mann. She'd had eight interviews and gotten five job offers. She was disappointed she didn't get eight offers. "I wonder if I should interview all over again?" she asked Mann. "How many jobs can you accept?" he reponded. "Just think about it and pick the best one." Peters spent a few years with that first firm but has spent the bulk of her career working in the energy industry in Houston. She established an endowed scholarship in Mann's name and has been very active with her alma mater over the years—she's served on the Texas Tech Alumni Association Board and the Rawls College of Business Advisory Board.

She's expecting a third generation of her family to become Red Raiders. "I would be proud to say we've had three generations to attend, particularly since we weren't able to attend the whole 100 years of Tech's existence," she said. She's also involved with Tech's Office of Diversity, Equity & Inclusion, working to help recruit students of color—"and others," she points out—and ensure they have a good support system and experience. "I had an overall good experience but wish there had been a better support system in place," she said.

Images courtesy of Texas Tech Communications and Marketing

Peters established an endowed scholarship in Mann's name and has been very active with her alma mater over the years—she's served on the Texas Tech Alumni Association Board and the Rawls College of Business Advisory Board.

Raider Red

Got one of them kits where ya mail in your DNA and they tell y'all where ya from.

Got it back. Said I'm 50 percent ink, 25 percent papier-mâché, and 25 percent chicken wire . . . which equals 100 percent West Texas awesome!

I know, y'all wish you were me.

I'm a national champion and have probably set a world record for high fives, hugs, and selfies. There are even beers named after me—which is great after an early season football game at the Jones. It gets purty steamy under my big hat and moustache.

I reckon I get around some. I was in Atlanta, 1993, when Coach Marsha Sharp led our women's basketball team to the natty. I was in the Jones, 2008, when Graham Harrell hit Michael Crabtree with that pass to beat the Longhorns. Now the secret can come out . . . I drew up the play. I was in Minneapolis, 2019, when our men's basketball team came within seconds of winning the national title. I'd like to say more about the officiating but don't want to get fined. I did help get us to the Final Four when I beat the Gonzaga Bulldog in a dance-off the week before in Anaheim.

A couple of years back, I won the Mascot Division in the National Cheerleaders Association and National Dance Alliance Collegiate Cheer and Dance Championships. In 2012, I won the Capital One Mascot Challenge and got a funny tale to tell 'bout that one. I was getting into an elevator to find out the final results and in walks country singer Dierks Bentley. He says, "Congratulations." I didn't know what he was talking about until the elevator door opened and I saw this big check for $20,000.

But my life ain't always big shindigs.

In October I visit endless elementary schools for college career week, which is great, because all the kids decide they want to be me! I also spend time consoling sick children and giving them a fun break.

Besides showing up at Texas Tech games I've been to Red Raider Orientation, business openings, fundraising events, parades—I was even at a presidential inauguration and was ring bearer at a wedding. I've been on Christmas ornaments, shirts, and bobbleheads. I love to twirl my guns, tip my hat to the ladies, and ring the Victory Bells! I work with our strength and conditioning staff because looking this great takes work.

People want to know where I live. It's a secret . . . but it's on campus. Got two roommates. One wears a mask and cape and is my older sibling. The other is a black horse. The horse has his own bathroom. Fortunately, we have a laundry room. Got to keep my white gloves looking bright!

Hard to keep up with my schoolwork because it's tough to type with your hands always in the Guns Up position. Because I work so hard for Tech they gave me a great major: Interdisciplinary Studies in School Spirit and Fun. I'm working on my dissertation on "1001 Ways to Cook Bevo."

I love movies, and my top five are: *Raiders of the Lost Ark*, *Tomb Raider*, *Red*, *Red 2*, and *Red Dawn*.

I know, y'all wish you were me.

Catherine Royalty

Catherine Royalty was born in Lubbock on February 17, 1915, to Walter "W. W." and Lyda May Royalty. One of her fondest memories was riding a bicycle up and down Broadway Avenue in the early 1920s as the red brick streets were laid connecting what would become College Avenue, later University Avenue, to the heart of downtown Lubbock where bustling shops, restaurants, and movie theaters congregated. Catherine witnessed more than a century of significant changes and challenges in her hometown, like those brick streets, as it cycled through boom periods of growth and expansion.

In 1923, a buzz of anticipation and energy swept through West Texas as efforts to bring a coeducational state college to the region finally came to fruition. With the passage of Texas Senate Bill No. 103, the Locating Board visited several possible sites for the new college, including Lubbock. Catherine's father, who owned one of the first car dealerships in town, loaned one of his automobiles to tour members of the Locating Board. Catherine's mother volunteered to serve as chauffeur for their company vehicle. The Royalty family were among the large crowd of revelers gathered downtown to hear Governor Pat Neff reaffirm the August 8 announcement that Lubbock was chosen. This very special memory of the founding of Texas Tech paved the way for Catherine and her mother to be among the group of women enrolled in the 1930s. While her mother, who worked in the campus post office, did not complete a degree, Catherine did, earning a bachelor's degree in English in June 1936.

Following graduation, she taught English and was a school librarian in Post. Catherine, whose family had a history of wartime military service, supported US efforts during World War II by selling bonds and distributing ration books.

Desiring to do more, she enlisted in the US Navy in the Women Accepted for Volunteer Emergency Service (WAVES), completed basic training in New York, and then worked in the secured fleet post office in San Francisco, tracking and communicating with US ships on active duty.

Honorably discharged from military service in February 1946, Catherine returned to Lubbock and reenrolled in Texas Tech under the GI Bill of Rights. She completed a master's degree in education in May 1951. Concurrently, Catherine taught English and journalism in various Lubbock middle schools. Experience gained working on *The Toreador* proved useful when Catherine established student newspapers at junior high schools Hutchinson, Atkins, O. L. Slaton, and Carroll Thompson and served in the role of newspaper adviser. In 1957, she authored a journalism handbook specifically for junior high students.

Catherine retired in 1977 after thirty-four years of teaching. She shared her inspirational life story with Texas Tech students in 2018 and threw out the first pitch at Texas Tech's 2019 Military Appreciation Softball Game. At age 105, Catherine was Lubbock's oldest World War II veteran and Texas Tech's oldest graduate at the time of her passing on May 15, 2020.

Images courtesy of Texas Tech Communications and Marketing

Dirk West

A group of mascots from the old Southwest Conference had a reunion recently at the Angry Dog in Dallas, a hop over Interstate 30 from the old conference's mecca—the Cotton Bowl. "I loved Dirk, except when he put holes in my hat," said the Red Raider. "I liked how when we were on a winning streak, Dirk drew me bigger and bigger," said the Baylor Bear. The Texas A&M Aggie started to tear up before he said, "He taught me how to spell 'duh.'"

Dirk West grew up in the Depression years watching Texas Tech football and stars like Tech's Elmer Tarbox and Tuffy Nabors, TCU's Sammy Baugh, and Hardin-Simmons' Bulldog Turner. He started drawing around kindergarten age and went on to become Lubbock's Renaissance Man—best known as the legendary cartoonist who created Raider Red. It started when West drew a cartoon for the *Lubbock Avalanche-Journal* in 1964 about Texas Tech playing powerhouse Texas. The strips became a weekly staple in the paper during football season, chronicling how the Red Raiders and other Southwest Conference teams were faring, coaching changes, and other issues.

There was the Red Raider, Baylor Bear, Texas Longhorn, A&M Aggie, Arkansas Razorback, Rice Owl, SMU Pony (Dirk spelled it SMEW), TCU Horned Frog, and Houston Cougar. Each loss added another bullet hole to Red's hat. Flies buzzed around the Razorback. The Cougar lived out of a trash can. And the Aggie cadet was "stoopid." West had other characters like Moss, Boo Bird, and Uncle Upright, who added to the frivolity. He had no problem teasing everyone—including Texas Tech, its Goin' Band, and the South Plains town of Muleshoe.

Fans in College Station warned West not to visit, but the threat only boosted his sense of humor. Once at a Tech–A&M game he saw a friend while standing near Aggie fans. He yelled at the buddy, "Hey, Dirk West!" The Aggie faithful threw food at his victim and booed. Texas Tech coach Jim Carlen got upset with West, telling the cartoonist he didn't understand the complexities of offensive football. West responded, "I don't know anything about the complexities of my TV set. But I know when it ain't working right. And what I know about your offense is that it ain't working right!"

Most SWC coaches enjoyed his work, however. "Without your cartoons to help keep this sport in perspective, we might mistake football for a serious business," said Arkansas coach Frank Broyles. West also brought the Red Raiders regional and national recognition, said Gerald Myers, former player, coach, and athletic director.

West and the *Avalanche-Journal*'s Burle Pettit had breakfast every morning in the newspaper's coffee shop. West's office was across the street. The two were great friends, but both had strong opinions and enjoyed arguing. The only time West was speechless was at a soiree when he retired from politics to which friends invited New York Yankees legend Mickey Mantle—West's hero.

West was looking forward to drawing cartoons for the Big 12 when he died of a heart attack in 1996 at age 66. "Lubbock has so few national treasures, and we have one less," said a friend about his passing. More than a quarter of a century later, his cartoons live on in memories, books, and on the wall of his grandson Cameron West's restaurant—Dirk's—in downtown Lubbock.

West's cartoons were featured on several TTU basketball programs over the years.
Images courtesy of Texas Tech Communications and Marketing

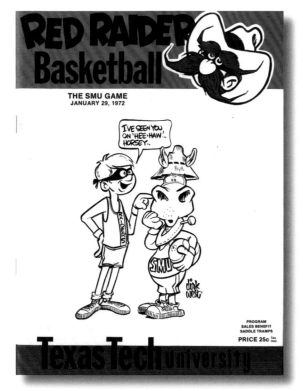

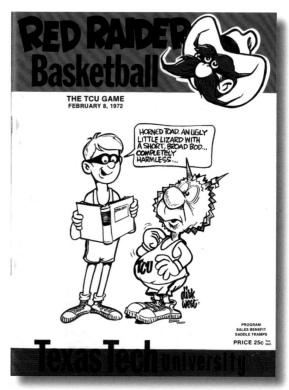

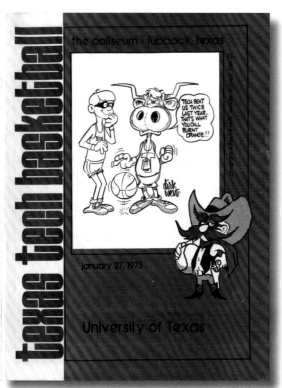

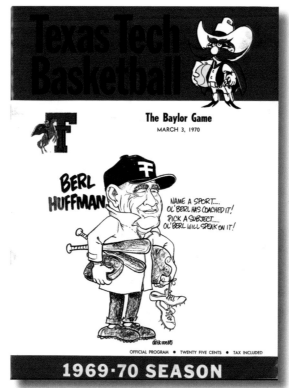

TEACHING

TEXAS TECH

Bill and Peggy Dean

Bill Dean is a legend. He was the first person EVER to switch on the lights for the Carol of Lights. He has told a hysterical (fictional) story about a young woman writing a letter home to her parents after her first semester at Texas Tech at every ring ceremony. He is and remains a difference-maker for generations of Red Raiders, past, present, and future, at Texas Tech University.

Many know Bill because he is synonymous with the Texas Tech Alumni Association (TTAA). As the president and CEO of the TTAA for forty years, he oversaw incredible growth and development of the alumni network. He was central to both the 1995 and 2008 expansion and renovation of the Texas Tech President's Home, where the TTAA has been housed since 1969, which was first renamed the Merket Alumni Center and then rechristened the McKenzie-Merket Alumni Center, and now holds the Peggy and Bill Dean Grand Reception Hall. He helped to facilitate the construction of the Frazier Alumni Pavilion in 1997 where alumni gather to celebrate game days before kickoff. For their incredible work in building the TTAA, Bill and Peggy were honored with the Lauro F. Cavazos Award by the Alumni Association in 2008.

When Bill announced his retirement as president and CEO of the TTAA in 2018 after forty years of leadership and dedication, alumni wondered aloud what they would do. Bill and Peggy *were* the Alumni Association. They had led with grace, style, good sense, and good humor. But in typical Dean fashion, Bill and Peggy had created an association with longevity and sustainability in mind. They built a legacy. They built a strong foundation. And the TTAA flourishes because Bill and Peggy believed in it, in its mission, in the promise that Texas Tech makes to it students and keeps in its alumni.

And worry not. Although Bill stepped down from his role with the TTAA, he is keeping himself busy. He is first and foremost a teacher. While he may no longer be Alumni Association president, he is still a professor. More than five decades in, he is still teaching mass communications, journalism, and public relations. And he is proving that he is still most worthy of all those awards he has won over the years: the President's Teaching Award for Excellence, the Texas Tech Parents Association Faculty Distinguished Leadership Award, the College of Media & Communication Outstanding Alumnus Award, the inaugural College of Media & Communication Lifetime Service Award, the Silver Addy Award from the Lubbock Chapter of the Federation of Advertising Executives, and the Heritage Award from the Double T Varsity Club.

And most recently, during the COVID-19 pandemic, Bill Dean—who started teaching when students still took notes using paper and pencil and who in those days wrote concepts in chalk on a green chalkboard—taught his first online course. Because five decades later, Bill is teaching the grandchildren of his original students, giving them a run for their money, cracking them up with his jokes, and challenging them to take full advantage of the enormous privilege of an educational experience at Texas Tech.

Left: Switching on the lights for the Carol of Lights ceremony in December 1960. The man pictured third from the left is Bill Dean and the one pictured at the far right is Texas Tech president R. C. Goodwin.

Images courtesy of the Southwest Collection / Special Collections Library

In typical Dean fashion, Bill and Peggy created an association with longevity and sustainability in mind. They built a legacy.

Mary Woodward Doak

Mary Woodward Doak's fifty-year career as a prominent Texas educator, counselor, and tireless champion of promoting and supporting women's academic achievement afforded her the lifelong affections of colleagues, students, alumni, and the Lubbock community alike. She was once eulogized as "a woman of wit, understanding, kindness, and intelligence," one who "probably influenced more South Plains women than any other at Tech."

Born on the Bar Bona Ranch in Live Oak County, Texas, on February 15, 1877, Woodward married Vernon Doak, a lawyer, in 1899. His untimely death and that of their young son galvanized her to pursue a full-time teaching career as a means for supporting herself and her two young daughters, Mary and Martha. From 1906 to 1917, Doak was employed as a high school teacher and assistant principal, then enrolled in the University of Texas where she earned bachelor's degrees in English and government in 1925 and was inducted into the honor society Phi Beta Kappa. She moved to Lubbock in 1925 as one of the first faculty members at Texas Technological College. Over the course of the next twenty-five years, Doak served as the first Dean of Women (from 1925 to 1945), acquired her master's degree in English and sociology from Texas Tech (1929), and taught in the English department until her retirement in 1950.

Several of Doak's contributions made a significant impact in the university's early role in educating women, particularly first-generation college attendees. She organized the first women's social club on campus, Las Chaparritas, in 1926 and the Texas Tech chapter of the Association of Women Students in 1929. She helped establish the Council of Women Graduates in 1927, which in turn helped the Lubbock chapter of the American Association of University Women become officially affiliated with the national association in 1949. The Forum, an honorary service organization for senior female students, was established in 1937 largely due to her efforts.

In cooperation with Margaret Weeks, dean of Home Economics, Doak inaugurated the Women's Recognition Service ceremony in 1932, which continued until 1947 with co-sponsorships by the Quarterly Club and the Association of Women Students. The Lubbock chapter of Delta Kappa Gamma established a scholarship in her name.

Women's Dormitory No. 1 was renamed by the Board of Regents in 1952 as Mary W. Doak Hall. It remains one of only four buildings on the Texas Tech main campus to be solely named after a woman. Additionally, Doak's visit to and subsequent lecture on the British Museum inspired the idea for establishing a museum at Texas Tech.

Professor Doak passed in her Lubbock home on April 20, 1952, following a two-year battle with pancreatic cancer. A large portrait of her by artist Emily Guthrie Smith was commissioned by the Quarterly Club and the Association of Women Student in 1947. The painting now resides in the Texas Tech University Archives at the Southwest Collection/Special Collections Library—a fitting home for the painting, given that Doak's daughter, Mary Wilson, was once employed as a curator there.

David Gaschen

Google map "from Hemmle Hall at Texas Tech University to the Broadway stage" and you'll see that it's a long drive; it also takes a lot determination, a wealth of talent, and a dreamer of no little dreams to make it.

A Lubbockite, David Gaschen graduated from Texas Tech with a degree in vocal performance in 1993 and moved to Chicago to build his professional career. He was recognized for his powerful voice, his immense stage presence, and his sensitivity as a performer and was cast in more than twenty musicals in the Windy City, including lead roles in Gilbert and Sullivan's *The Pirates of Penzance* and Romberg and Donnelly's *The Student Prince*.

By May 1995, in Basel, Switzerland, he was named the alternate for the Phantom in Andrew Lloyd Webber's critically acclaimed and award-winning *The Phantom of the Opera*. David would perform three to four times a week in the title role and, at age twenty-six, became the youngest performer who played the Phantom in a professional production. And to top it all off, he originally sang the role in German. He was soon cast as the lead in the German production of *Phantom* in Hamburg. David Gaschen performed the role of the Phantom over a thousand times in Europe.

During one of those thousand performances, in summer 1999, David found himself singing for famed Broadway producer Harold Prince, who immediately cast him in the title role on Broadway where David would debut in November. He made an indelible mark on Broadway as the Phantom and is included in "Broadway's Fabulous Phantoms" with the likes of Howard McGillin, Hugh Panaro, and Michael Crawford. After several years on Broadway, David decided to become a recording artist and perform in concert arenas. He has recorded two solo CDs and a Christmas album that have afforded him invitations to perform with the Fairfax Symphony Orchestra, the Wheeling Symphony Orchestra, the Lubbock Symphony Orchestra, the Allen Philharmonic Orchestra, the Dallas Symphony Orchestra, the Longview Symphony Orchestra, and internationally with the Jalisco Philharmonic Orchestra in Guadalajara, Mexico.

In 2006, David was inducted onto the West Texas Walk of Fame honoring West Texans who have excelled in the arts. He returned to Lubbock to receive the Distinguished Alumni Award from the Texas Tech University Alumni Association in 2018. He is a frequent visitor to Lubbock, not least because he believes firmly in giving back. In an interview with KCBD, David revealed, "I had a few of those instances when I was at Tech, where my voice teachers and the teachers at Tech would bring in someone who had done something in the arts and outside of Lubbock. I always said to myself, if I ever had the chance, I would want to come back to Lubbock and show them if you really work hard and you pay your dues and you study hard, it will pay off in the future."

In 2016, David returned to Texas Tech to reprise the role of the Phantom in a benefit. Playing opposite a Texas Tech student in the role of Christine—Honors College and J. T. and Margaret Talkington College of Visual & Performing Arts student Marissa Hernandez (who would go on to graduate from TTU and earn a Master of Music in Vocal Performance at the New York University Tisch School of Performing Arts)—David Gaschen proves that the Phantom looms large over all of us, giving us joy and music and, in the end, freedom in the voice of a Texas Tech graduate.

Image courtesy of David Gaschen

David became the youngest performer who played the Phantom in a professional production. And to top it all off, he originally sang the role in German.

Elizabeth G. "Bess" Haley

Born on July 30, 1944, Elizabeth Haley left her hometown of Homer, Louisiana, to attend nearby Louisiana Tech University. Her father, F. C. Haley, Superintendent of Claiborne Parish, and her mother, Gladys Murphy Haley, a high school teacher, encouraged their three offspring to pursue college degrees that would provide them meaningful careers. Brothers Robert and Benjamin set out for medical school while Bess chose to pursue a career in academia. After earning a bachelor's degree in home economics in 1966, she attended Florida State University, from which she received a master's degree in clothing and textiles in 1968 and a doctoral degree in child development in 1972.

She began teaching at Louisiana Tech University in 1969 as an instructor and director of the nursery school, rising to the rank of dean and professor by 1975. The selection of Dr. Haley in 1981 as incoming dean marked a new era of revitalization for Texas Tech's College of Home Economics. Under her guidance and leadership, the college was renamed Human Sciences in 1993, student enrollment increased and faculty research expanded, and new programs were established for Restaurant, Hotel and Institutional Management (RHIM), family financial planning, and substance abuse studies. Notable upticks in student scholarships, college endowments, and alumni relations during the 1980s and 1990s are additionally attributed to Haley. From 1981 to 1982, she served as president of the National Council of Administrators of Home Economics and was named by the American Home Economics Association (now the American Association of Family & Consumer Sciences) in 1985 as one of the nation's top ten "Home Economics to Watch."

In 1988, Dr. Haley became the first woman appointed at Texas Tech to take charge of presidential duties who also had the full academic credentials for such a high-level university position. When asked about being the first woman to cross that barrier, she replied, "I feel it is important for women faculty members and women students at Texas Tech. But I feel both men and women can serve effectively in a wide variety of jobs." She resumed being dean the next year, stepping away from the role in 2000.

Haley's impressive administrative track record resulted in her appointment as deputy chancellor for operations for the Texas Tech University System in 2001, with a subsequent transfer to Institutional Advancement for eleven years. Although retired in 2014 following the passing of her husband, Dr. Glenn Murray Jones, Haley accepted Chancellor Robert Duncan's invitation in 2015 to serve as a special adviser for fundraising efforts in the College of Visual & Performing Arts. Her evident strength in the areas of donor relations and fundraising made Haley a natural choice for development efforts needed in the procurement of expanded facilities and vital resources for the flourishing college. She retired again on May 31, 2019.

As of 2021, Dr. Elizabeth Haley is the only woman on the Texas Tech campus to serve as professor, dean, interim president, and deputy chancellor for operations.

Donald Haragan

The Honors College honored Don Haragan by naming one of its four Harry Potter–style houses after the former professor, chair, associate dean, interim dean, provost, vice president, president, and interim chancellor of Texas Tech University. Quite rightly, Haragan House is dedicated to the pillar of service, for the person who, for more than forty years, led this university in virtually every leadership role available. In fact, on the walls of the Honors conference room named for Dr. Haragan is the house shield that bears his name—and a list of every single office in every single academic building he occupied, with next to it a hilarious map of every corresponding parking spot. On the feature wall is a photo of Dr. Haragan taken by one of his biggest admirers and mentees, former dean of the Honors College, Dr. Michael San Francisco, showing him doing what he loved most—teaching.

Haragan received his BS and PhD from the University of Texas and his MS from Texas A&M. He focused his undergraduate and master's degrees in meteorology and received his doctorate in civil engineering in a program of engineering science. After he experienced those *other* Texas schools, he made his way to Lubbock, where he found his home at Texas Tech in 1969 when he joined the Department of Geosciences as the very first faculty-member atmospheric science professor at Texas Tech University. His colleagues and peers soon realized that he was not only an outstanding scholar and teacher but a born leader, someone who could bring people together. And in every single leadership position, he found new ways to expand the reach of Texas Tech and believe in its potential as an institution that could promote research, entrepreneurship, creative activity, scholarship, and undergraduate and graduate education.

For Dr. Haragan, that meant encouraging students to understand that the local is global and the global is local. During his time as an administrator, he opened the Texas Tech Center in Seville, Spain. He insisted that to learn another culture was to discover more about yourself, your place, your own home. He believed fundamentally in the possibilities of education and helped to increase the number of international students at Texas Tech through concerted recruitment efforts and by working to create a campus that would welcome people of all perspectives, experiences, and areas of expertise.

It was this insistence on open-mindedness that led Dr. Haragan to found an Honors College that brought together students of all majors, interests, and passions and inspire them to pursue a breadth, depth, and profundity of education through the study of the arts, humanities, science, technology, engineering, and mathematics. As Haragan described his hope for the Honors College, "It's a different kind of experience. All the colleges are represented; the students are highly motivated and the students work together." Haragan insisted that to build Texas Tech into a nationally renowned, world-class university and to move it into Tier One status, the institution could not focus its efforts only on research and the graduate programs while slighting undergraduate education.

Perhaps that is why, when Dr. Haragan stepped down from his administrative positions, he chose to return to the Honors College as an atmospheric science professor. While Haragan wore every hat, held every title, lived in every office, and parked in every spot at Texas Tech University, the role and identity he holds most dear is that of professor and educator. And his heart remains, always, with the students.

Top: Image courtesy of the Southwest Collection / Special Collections Library
Bottom: Image courtesy of Michael San Francisco

Haragan House is dedicated to the pillar of service, for the person who, for more than forty years, led this university in virtually every leadership role available.

Katharine Hayhoe

Katharine Hayhoe is a champion of the earth. Period. Full stop.

There are few like her in the world. And here she is, in Lubbock, at Texas Tech. Championing the world from the South Plains and bringing her own inimitable brand of rigor, intelligence, wit, faith, and approachability to the science of climate change. Whether it's teaching, giving public talks, writing books, or sitting between Leonardo DiCaprio and Barack Obama shooting the breeze on the south lawn of the White House, Katharine Hayhoe is energy efficient—and effective.

Hayhoe continues to have these same conversations with anyone and everyone who will engage—with the curious high school student, the doubting politician, the ambitious undergraduate, and the concerned members of any faith, but particularly those Christians who are looking for answers, looking for ways forward.

She is a Paul Whitfield Horn Distinguished Professor and the Political Science Endowed Chair in Public Policy and Public Law in the Department of Political Science at Texas Tech University as well as an associate in the Public Health program of the Graduate School of Biomedical Sciences at the Texas Tech University Health Sciences Center. She is a prolific author, an internationally renowned scholar, and an award-winning teacher. She is also a writer and producer for the *Global Weirding: Climate, Politics, and Religion* series with Texas Tech Public Media and is widely sought out as an expert voice in documentaries and film.

Her reach is global, just like her research area. She is the Chief Scientist for The Nature Conservancy. She serves on the Executive Summary Committee and was a convening and lead author of several chapters in the first two volumes of the US Global Change Research Program's Fourth National Climate Assessment. And she is the critically acclaimed author of *Saving Us: A Climate Scientist's Case for Hope and Healing in a Divided World*, that has been embraced by scholars, activists, political leaders, and influencers alike. In 2014, Katharine was named one of the 100 Most Influential People by *TIME* magazine and one of the 100 Leading Global Thinkers by *Foreign Policy* (she received this honor again in 2019). In 2015, she was recognized as one of 20 Climate Champions by *The Huffington Post* and in 2016, she received the Distinguished Service Award from the Sierra Club, the Friend of the Planet Award from the National Center for Science Education, and was listed as one of the most influential visionaries in transforming American politics by *POLITICO 50*. In 2017, *Fortune* honored her as one of the world's greatest leaders, and in 2018, she was named a YWCA Woman of Excellence in Science. And in 2019, she was named the United Nations Champion of the Earth for Science and Innovation.

With all these accolades, for which she is most humbly grateful and still very much surprised, she is still Katharine. Her head has not gotten as big as these West Texas skies. She still makes time to respond to emails, answer the questions of children, be a teacher of students. As she explains, her work is not about herself. She has to remember what her purpose is: "As a Christian, I believe we're called to love others as we've been loved by God, and that means caring for those who are suffering—their physical needs and their well-being—which today are being exacerbated by climate impacts. How could I not want to do something about that?"

Images courtesy of Texas Tech Marketing and Communications

Judi Henry

Judi Henry has changed more student lives than one can imagine. That is because, at heart, regardless of what position she held at Texas Tech, she has been an educator. So whether she was the dean of students and assistant vice president for student affairs or the senior associate athletics director and senior woman administrator for the Department of Intercollegiate Athletics or an adjunct instructor in kinesiology and sport management at TTU or a middle school teacher at Smylie Wilson, she was always first and foremost a mentor, a guide, an adviser, a teacher, someone who knew that she would shape young minds and influence their futures.

That is partially because she herself had some wonderful and supportive teachers. And that is mostly because she knows just how much young people need someone like her, someone with expertise, intelligence, empathy, compassion. Someone who seeks solutions. Someone who blazes trails. Someone who clears the path for the next generation.

For over forty years, Judi Henry has done just that. Whether it was busting down doors for gender equity, ensuring the proper implementation of Title IX, or challenging those who would prevent the inclusion of those who have waited for far too long for the playing field to be leveled, Dr. Henry was the champion of us all.

Wielding three degrees from Texas Tech, Henry has been an essential part of the history of diversity, equity, and inclusion at the university. As dean of students, she was engaged in the weighty discussions among students and faculty. And she was an insistent voice as the Faculty Senate approved a Multicultural Core graduation requirement that would introduce all students to the extensive vocabulary of living in a diverse global society.

When Henry moved to Athletics in 1997, she continued the work of Jeannine McHaney who, in 1975, became the first director of Women's Athletics at Texas Tech and who, in turn, hired Marsha Sharp in 1982 to be the new head coach of the Lady Raiders basketball program. Henry worked diligently to implement Title IX requirements and make available equal opportunities for women athletes.

As senior associate commissioner of the Big 12 Conference Dru Hancock describes her, "Simply put, Dr Judi Henry is one of the finest, most respected administrators with whom I have ever worked. She is admired and beloved by so many of her colleagues at the Big 12 conference and national levels. [S]he has mentored so many young professionals, and they have benefited from her wisdom. She is one of the warmest, most sincere individuals our profession has ever had."

Dr. Henry was able to do all this because she focused on her relationships her entire tenure at Texas Tech. Because this was never a job for her. This was home. This was family. And it always will be for this Red Raider through and through.

Images courtesy of the Southwest Collection / Special Collections Library

At heart, regardless of what position Henry held at Texas Tech, she has been an educator.

Paul Whitfield Horn

Paul Whitfield Horn, Texas Tech's first president, was a tireless intellectual who built a remarkable career in education and a dynamic early reputation for a fledgling Texas Technological College. Born in Boonville, Missouri, Horn graduated from Boonville High School at the age of fourteen and four years later received an MA degree from Central College, a Methodist school in nearby Fayette. He entered teaching, and education became his profession.

He married Maud Keith in 1890. They had one child, Ruth, who later wrote a book on Texas Technological College's first thirty years of operation. Ambitious, determined, and always seeking more favorable opportunities, Horn moved from one teaching position to another. He and Maud located to Texas in 1892. In his adopted state, Horn served as a principal and then superintendent at such schools as Valley View and Belcherville before becoming superintendent of Sherman Public Schools, a position he held from 1897 to 1904. Then he became superintendent of schools in Houston.

In Houston, Horn gained a national reputation for his influence on education. He published *Our Schools Today* (1908), *School Room Essentials* (1911), and *Best Things in Our Schools* (1914), plus a series of readers and a spelling book. Perhaps his most recognized contribution to public education was the development of "the junior high school plan." Such work got him the presidency of the Texas State Teachers Association in 1910 and vice president of the National Education Association. It also earned him honorary doctorates from Baylor University, Southwestern University, and from his alma mater Central College.

Dr. Horn left Houston in 1921 for an educational position in Mexico City, but a year later returned to Texas to become president of Southwestern University in Georgetown. When Texas Technological College opened in 1925, Horn became its first president. Aiming to build the new school's reputation and supported by an effective Board of Directors, which was chaired by domineering Amon Carter, Horn went to work. He oversaw student recruitment, encouraged the efforts of school and grounds architect William Ward Watkin, and hired several truly outstanding and visionary professors, including William Curry Holden in history and anthropology and Leroy Thompson Patton in geology, both of whom gained national reputations.

Horn was a promoter. With student enrollment surprisingly high, he pushed for an addition to the administration building, another classroom building, a separate library building, and a gymnasium. He meant to expand the university. He encouraged a strong "town and gown" relationship, and to achieve it, he joined a local service club. Also, he often attended the weekly meeting of the influential Rotary Club of Lubbock. He usually brought with him to the Wednesday Rotary Club gathering such members of the Board of Directors as Clifford B. Jones, R. A. Underwood, and J. E. Nunn.

Horn was also a man of faith. He taught Sunday school each week at First Methodist Church, attended services there, and sought to establish a college-age Methodist Wesley Foundation program on the campus. Paul Whitfield Horn died in April 1932, near the end of the spring semester during his seventh year as president of Texas Technological College, an institution whose reputation, owing to his vision and industry, he had set on solid ground.

Ernst Kiesling

Ernst Kiesling had become chair of the university's civil engineering department the year before the 1970 Lubbock tornado killed twenty-six people. He and four other Texas Tech professors—Kishor Mehta, Joe Minor, Jim McDonald, and Richard Peterson—started studying wind damage and eventually created the National Wind Institute. The quintet worked together, but each had their areas of expertise. Kiesling was looking at tornado damage in Burnet, Texas, a few years after the deadly Lubbock storm. A house was almost completely destroyed, its roof gone and walls missing. What was left had holes in it from flying debris, but in the center of the kitchen was a small room—a pantry—still standing.

What if they could create a small room inside a home—a safe place during severe weather? Being small, such a space could be economical. Some people had below-ground storm shelters but couldn't always get to them. The professors got some two-by-four lumber, since that's what did a lot of damage when ripped from houses during tornadoes. How fast did it travel? And what could be built to stop it?

Kiesling and his colleagues decided a 15-pound two-by-four could have been carried by 250-mile-per-hour winds, which would have hurtled the lumber 100 miles per hour. They replicated that condition by dropping the wood off the top of the Architecture Building (now Media and Communication) just east of Urbanovsky Park. Kiesling referred to the timber as missiles. From the experiments, the professors learned that two layers of plywood weren't enough protection. They added more plywood. Even when the plywood was thick enough, they learned, the missiles could still do damage where the plywood was joined. Two layers of plywood and a metal sheet would stop the missiles.

They further learned that reinforced concrete blocks worked well for commercial construction. The engineers improved their processes, creating a launching device to hurtle the lumber that Kiesling jokingly called a big potato gun. These experiments would save lives, but the man leading the initiative could easily have walked a different path.

"Ernie"—as his colleagues called him—wasn't planning on going to college, let alone teaching. Growing up in San Angelo, he thought he'd farm, living on land east of town after he graduated from high school. He saw a school bus go by and thought maybe he should try college for a semester even though he had no idea what he wanted to do. Kiesling was good at math and was guided into a pre-engineering curriculum at San Angelo College—which eventually became Angelo State University. He went on to Tech, where he was intrigued by an engineering class in dynamics—the reaction of bodies to forces. His teacher was J. H. Murdough, whom Kiesling called a "Texas Tech legend," chair of civil engineering and now with a dorm named for him. Murdough opened the teaching door to Kiesling. He liked it—eventually chairing the same department.

Kiesling helped organize the Lubbock-based National Storm Shelter Association, which has set building standards for the safe havens. The association is working on shelters for schools. The Federal Emergency Management Agency has published guidebooks on shelter construction and credits Kiesling as the father of the safe room. "That's an honor I really cherish," said Kiesling in an interview shortly before he passed away at age 87 in 2021. He credits "leadership from above" for his career. "I often found myself in opportune positions and I view it as an act of God," he said.

Image courtesy of the Southwest Collection / Special Collections Library

Kiesling helped organize the Lubbock-based National Storm Shelter Association, which has set building standards for the safe havens.

Dean Killion

Dean Killion didn't start the Goin' Band from Raiderland; that was Harry Lemaire, who also wrote "The Matador Song." Killion didn't put the band on the map; that was "Prof." D. O. Wiley, known as the father of bands in Texas, who came from Hardin-Simmons. What Killion did do was take the band on a crescendo journey with his precision-marching show band, creating innovative marching band designs, the concepts of the "foot and a half," and Band 1 and Band 2.

He also recruited and inspired a young man from Hale Center to join the band. "I wanted to be like Dean Killion," said Keith Bearden, who went on to be the first Goin' Band member to become its director. Bearden retired in 2003. At that point, the two of them had led the band forty-four years—more than half of Texas Tech's then-78 years.

Killion was born in Nebraska and started taking drum lessons when he was four. He joined his local city band, which played in a collective of different bands in Tulsa, Oklahoma, under the direction of John Philip Sousa. He began playing trumpet in seventh grade and then added cornet. Killion received a bachelor's degree in music education and a Master of Music degree from the University of Nebraska. From 1951 to 1959 he held various music jobs before he and wife Pat—also a Nebraska music major—came to Lubbock.

Under Killion's leadership from 1959 to 1980 as director of bands, the Goin' Band doubled in size to more than 400 and built on its reputation as one of the best college bands in the country. "Anyone who contends there's a better band in the country will get an argument from me," said a Philadelphia viewer in a series of comments collected by Killion's friends. "The TV announcers who see many of the fine bands throughout the football season also claimed this to be the best they have seen," said an Ohioan.

Killion started the Court Jesters band for Red Raider basketball games. There were also four concert bands and three stage bands. He grew the Summer Band Camp. The stars were the students who most people saw marching during Texas Tech football games, playing well-known favorites like "Fight Raiders, Fight," "March Grandioso," and "The Matador Song." Killion created the "foot and a half" to keep band members from wandering around. "He'd say get in your foot and a half, which meant your spot on the field. You kept one foot in place, you could roam 18 inches," said Bearden. Killion had grids on paper made into tablets to plan out his precision shows. He also created Band 1 and Band 2—matching bands playing on either side of the 50-yard line to create stereophonic sound. Even though each band is a mirror image of the other, a fierce debate has existed over time between Band 1 and Band 2 as to who's better.

Killion also changed the band's look, moving away from the Spanish-style Matador uniforms toward a more Big Ten look—a high hat with a plume and a military-looking coat with breastplate and long tail. The band members wore spats over their shoes. When Bearden took over, he returned to the Spanish-influenced look—but he kept the spats.

Killion retired from teaching in 1985 but continued to conduct the Lubbock Westwinds Community Brass Band he founded in 1960 until shortly before his death. Killion battled several health issues before he passed away in 1997. The Goin' Band wore black ribbons in his honor during the football game that year against Kansas State.

Lloyd Maines

At almost every Lubbock Lights concert since its inception in 2015 there has been a constant on stage—he doesn't always talk much, he doesn't want to be the featured star, but very clearly, he is the one to whom all the other artists look, in whom they find their rhythm. Lloyd Maines may not seek the spotlight, but he is the heart and soul of the band. And quite clearly, the other artists who have graced the stage of the Allen Theatre to celebrate the best music that West Texas has to offer—like Wade Bowen, Terry Allen, Joe Ely, Amanda Shires, Bob Livingston, and so many more—embrace him as their ringleader.

While Lloyd Maines has never forgotten his Lubbock roots, his reach far extends that of the South Plains, and over the past 40-plus years, Lloyd has shared his talents with the world as a Grammy Award–winning producer and musician. Find yourself a great album recorded by a Texas artist or produced in the Lone Star State and, most likely, you'll find Lloyd's fingerprints all over it. He is a producer extraordinaire, an exceptional pedal-steel player, and he can sing both lead and harmonies like a Rat Pack crooner. And of course, like so many talented musicians, he comes from a von Trapp–like family that has grown up singing and performing together, the much beloved Maines Brothers Band (that was first founded by the father and uncle of Lloyd but eventually became the new name of the Little Maines Brothers Band made up of Lloyd, Donnie, Kenny, and Steve Maines). And of course, that musicality was passed down to the next generation as Lloyd's daughter, Natalie, the lead singer of the Dixie Chicks, called upon her father's expertise for the Country Music Award–winning album *Wide Open Spaces.*

Born and raised in Lubbock, Texas, Lloyd attended Texas Tech majoring in forestry and thinking that he would get a job in the parks department. Life had other plans for him. He got into the recording studio and there was no turning back for him. He met Joe Ely at a bar in Lubbock, got him to play harmonica for a gospel project, and all of a sudden, Lloyd was part of the band. The goal was to make enough gas money to get to Austin. They played a few gigs, with no rehearsal, and the crowd went wild. So Joe didn't go to Austin right away and Lloyd played on his first four albums. They even went on tour with the English punk band The Clash, when being on the road just wasn't as much fun. Lloyd then began concentrating on the studio.

Soon Terry Allen came calling. Terry wanted to record an album called *Lubbock (on everything)* and he wanted to cut the album in Lubbock. And if there was anyone who could do the work in Lubbock, it was Lloyd Maines. He ended up helping people get their songs on tape, everything from country to rock to conjunto. And he loved it. Self-taught, part-psychologist, part-engineer, part-wizard, Lloyd helped some of the most famous artists find exactly the right chorus, exactly the right tone, exactly the right feel.

Maybe that's why on that stage for Lubbock Lights, all the artists immediately turn *toward* Lloyd instinctually when they play. Because they know that he is their North Star who will help hone their voice and guide them home. Because he is, of course, our own Lubbock Light.

Over the past 40-plus years, Lloyd has shared his talents with the world as a Grammy Award-winning producer and musician.

Wyman Meinzer

Wyman Meinzer is no stranger to the road. He knows how the sun sets the sky aflame in fuchsia and lavender at just the right time on just the right evenings. He knows how the wind blows particles from the Arctic across the plains and we breathe in the vestiges of times long past. He knows how the critters, big and small, can stand motionless against the desertscapes and how, when they sense danger or prairie fire or tornado, they can rise en masse and take flight, whether they be four-legged or two-legged or no-legged or winged. He knows how to find the beauty in what so many others see as unbeautiful. He is a photographer.

He knows these landscapes because he was raised on League Ranch, a 27,000-acre property in Knox County on the plains of Texas. And he has, inspired by these expanses of space, explored the corners of the state, learning the land, the people, the animals, and the vegetation with awe, respect, and humility. Meinzer is the only official State Photographer in Texas, named by the 1997 Texas State Legislature and then Governor George W. Bush.

Meinzer first arrived at Texas Tech determined to study coyotes. One of his professors loaned him a 35mm camera so he could do his research on the diet of coyotes, and while he completed that project, it wasn't the data that inspired him so much as looking through that lens and seeing the land that he loved so much from a completely different frame. When he graduated from Texas Tech in 1974 with a degree in wildlife management from the College of Agricultural Sciences and Natural Resources, he took the next three years living among the animals, studying and photographing them. In an interview, he described, "I was out there for weeks at a time with no other person. I had thousands of acres to roam over freely, and I could see all kinds of gorgeous sights and weather patterns. I got to be a student at a very basic level once again."

The student also served as the teacher. Meinzer taught as an adjunct instructor for twelve years and was awarded the Agricultural Communications Teacher of the Year in 2005. But he was not held by the four walls of a classroom and, after graduation, he worked as a professional predator hunter while training his eye and learning how to lens the land he loved.

For more than three decades, Meinzer has inspired people across the world with his transformative images. He has contributed photos to and/or written more than two dozen large-format books, and his works have been featured on more than 250 magazine covers. His pieces have been seen in *Smithsonian* magazine, *National Geographic* books, *Natural History*, *Ebony*, *Time*, *Newsweek*, *U.S. News & World Report*, *Audubon*, *Field & Stream*, and many more. And he has won numerous awards for his stunning photographs, including the John Ben Shepperd Jr. Award from the Texas Historical Foundation, The Conservation Society of San Antonio's Historic Preservation Award for the natural history book *Roadrunner*, the 2003 Star of Texas Award from the Gillespie County Historical Society, and the A. C. Greene Award, presented to a distinguished Texas author for lifetime achievement.

Perhaps the highest praise, beyond all these awards and accolades, is the description by David Baxter, former editor of *Texas Parks & Wildlife* magazine, of Meinzer as "a man with the eye of a nineteenth-century impressionist painter and the soul of a buffalo hunter."

Left: Photo by Coy F. Harris
Right: Photo by Sylinda Meinzer

For more than three decades, Meinzer has inspired people across the world with his transformative images.

Paul Milosevich

Paul Milosevich was talking to a friend in the mid-1970s, saying he was thinking of quitting his job teaching art at Texas Tech University. The friend was Jerry Allison, drummer for the Crickets, who co-wrote some of the band's biggest hits with his friend Buddy Holly in the late 1950s. Milosevich had a paycheck and tenure and enjoyed teaching—but academia was too constricting, a collar two sizes too small. "There ain't no such thing as security," Allison told him. "You might as well do something you like to do."

Milosevich left Texas Tech as an employee and went on to a successful life as a portrait painter with a studio in Santa Fe. For someone who taught at the university for only a few years, his brushstrokes are all over campus in portraits: Lady Raider legend Sheryl Swoopes in United Supermarkets Arena; Gene Hemmle outside Hemmle Hall in the School of Music; Jerry Rawls at the Rawls Course. There are, the artist estimates, around seventy-five of his portraits on campus and endless more across the country and world.

Milosevich grew up in a Trindad, Colorado, farmhouse with no electricity or indoor plumbing after his family emigrated from Croatia. He fell in love with golf, working as a caddy in his hometown before getting college degrees at California State University, Long Beach in Southern California. Milosevich taught art at Odessa College, two hours south of Lubbock. He joined Texas Tech's School of Art in 1970 as Two-Dimensional Coordinator—a fancy title, he thought—focusing on painting, drawing, printmaking, and commercial art.

The School of Art was next to the Architecture Building, where musicians would play during lunchtime. That's where Milosevich met the Flatlanders—Joe Ely, Jimmie Dale Gilmore, and Butch Hancock. He liked the music, and even though making a living as a musician was not easy, he liked how much fun they had. Milosevich started going to the Main Street Saloon, Fat Dogs, and the Cotton Club, following Ely and others. He loved the Sunday night jams at Stubb's Bar-B-Q in east Lubbock. Around this time, he also met country singer-songwriter Tom T. Hall and confided in Hall about going off on his own. The man who wrote a dozen No. 1 songs told Milosevich if he left teaching, Hall would keep him busy doing paintings for his Nashville home. It also opened a door for Milosevich to do charcoal portraits of inductees to the Nashville Songwriters Hall of Fame. Milosevich did album cover artwork for Hall, the Crickets, and Ely.

Another reason Milosevich chafed inside Tech's School of Art was that most of the faculty were partial to abstract work while he preferred the real world of portraits. That predilection came from a love of people, connecting them especially. "One of my hobbies is introducing people," he said. Milosevich introduced Hall to Ely and Stubb (C. W. Stubblefield), which led to Hall's song "The Great East Broadway Onion Championship of 1978," where Hall and Ely played pool with an onion from Stubb's kitchen. "I like everybody," said Milosevich. "I gravitate toward people I find something in common with, and in Lubbock the most interesting people were the musicians in the '70s and '80s."

Top right: Image courtesy of the Southwest Collection / Special Collections Library.
Left and bottom right: Images courtesy of Paul Milosevich.

Sunanda Mitra

When Rita Mitra's mother died—trailblazing physicist / electrical engineer Sunanda Mitra—Rita was the last surviving person in her immediate family. But she was not alone. "I had all these siblings supporting me—my mother's students," she said about the 2020 funeral services held on Zoom during the COVID pandemic. A year later, Rita got a note from one of her mom's former Texas Tech students who put Sunanda Mitra's photo on his family's Día de los Muertos altar.

Sunanda Mitra is remembered as a sweet, gracious, optimistic, and loving parent figure for many students. "She really made an impact," said Rita, adding that her mother would financially support students, put them as first authors on publications, invite them to the Mitra family's home. She was also brilliant—marrying physics and electrical engineering to lead to digital imaging breakthroughs for medicine and image recognition.

Mitra's journey started in her native India, where was fascinated by physics after reading *The Mysterious Universe*. Her older brother said girls didn't study physics. She insisted. He relented. After bachelor's and master's degrees in physics from the University of Calcutta, she began working on her doctorate. Her husband Arun was invited to pursue his doctorate in Germany. She eventually joined him there and finished hers. While in Germany, she was inspired by the work of Maria Goeppert Mayer, who won a Nobel Prize for discovering nuclear shell structure.

The couple planned to go back to India, but Arun heard about a mathematics faculty position opening at Texas Technological College. The Mitras arrived in Lubbock in 1967.

Mitra did work at the university and on human vision at Texas Tech's Health Sciences Center. That work led to a visiting faculty position at New York's Mount Sinai School of Medicine in 1983. A year later she became the first female faculty member in electrical engineering, which she learned in her late 40s. "Now it's no big deal" to have women in electrical engineering, said Brian Nutter, one of her students and now a faculty member. "But she faced a lot of inertia." Her daughter said, "It was very difficult for women of her generation to be heard." Mitra pushed forward in her sweet, tenacious way, saying, years later, "I don't think there are gender barriers anymore. If you want to, if you're interested, then you can do anything."

She was one of the first people doing image processing. The personal computer was just coming into use. She brought in high-end computers and connected cameras to get digital imaging long before webcams existed. Mitra worked with Texas Instruments and Northrop Grumman, advising them on image recognition.

Dozens of her students took what she taught them and went on to make devices and write algorithms used across many different platforms for digital image recognition. Mitra, with others, developed the Texas Tech Neuroimaging Institute and was also an adjunct professor in the former TTUHSC Department of Radiology. Later, she was involved in research on identifying cancerous brain tissue and discovering how our brains work. Mitra was a Horn Professor, among many other honors. Her strengths, said her daughter, were her curiosity and the ability to see both the big picture and the details.

Mitra established the Dr. Atindra Mitra Graduate Fellowship in Electrical and Computer Engineering to her honor her son, who got his bachelor's, master's, and doctoral degrees in electrical engineering, all from Texas Tech.

Top right and bottom images courtesy of Texas Tech Communications and Marketing

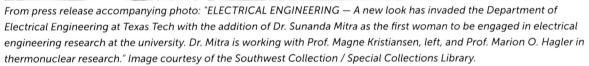

From press release accompanying photo: "ELECTRICAL ENGINEERING — A new look has invaded the Department of Electrical Engineering at Texas Tech with the addition of Dr. Sunanda Mitra as the first woman to be engaged in electrical engineering research at the university. Dr. Mitra is working with Prof. Magne Kristiansen, left, and Prof. Marion O. Hagler in thermonuclear research." Image courtesy of the Southwest Collection / Special Collections Library.

Grover E. Murray

Grover Murray's secretary said Roy Furr from Lubbock, Texas, was on the phone. Furr told Murray—then academic vice president at Louisiana State University—that he represented Texas Technological College's Board of Directors. "We're looking for a new president. Your name has been recommended and we'd like to come talk to you," he told Murray on that mid-1960s day. A contingent from Lubbock traveled to Baton Rouge.

Their vision impressed Murray—making Texas Tech a top academic and research institution. They also wanted more successful athletic programs to showcase the university.

Murray eventually agreed to become Texas Tech's eighth president for $35,000 a year, plus house and car. The compensation package seemed tremendous at the time, said Murray years later in an interview. He came to Lubbock with his wife Nancy and two daughters.

After ten years, Murray left the president's role. What had been Texas Technological College was now Texas Tech University. He shoved the school onto the trajectory the Board of Directors sought—which his successors have followed. "It was not a simple thing we were trying to do. I had to step on some toes; you can't pamper everybody," he said. After arriving, Murray asked for undated resignations from deans, vice presidents, and other high-ranking Tech officials. It was an old academic custom, but it was also the start of some house-cleaning. Murray wanted to bring in as much new blood and thinking as he could.

This included athletics. Texas Tech had recently joined the Southwest Conference after a few decades in the Border Conference. Murray felt the Red Raiders still had a "Border Conference mentality and needed a Southwest Conference mentality." Anything other than a clean program was unacceptable. If a coach did anything "under the table—don't wait for me to fire you, just pack your bags and leave," he said. Murray also made it clear he wanted people in athletics to talk to him and "not someone in the game room at the Lubbock Club." During Murray's tenure, J. T. King moved up to the post of athletics director, and Tech hired Jim Carlen as football coach. Carlen went 37–20–2 in five seasons, the best being an 11–1 record in 1973, ending with a Gator Bowl win.

Looking for ways to get Texas Tech national recognition beyond the playing fields, Murray realized the school could not compete, for example, with the University of Chicago in mathematics or Stanford in engineering. Given the arid climate of West Texas, Murray started the International Center for Arid and Semiarid Land Studies, which has gone on to partner with institutions around the world in other arid environments. A lot more happened on Murray's watch: the medical and law schools opened, along with the university museum. Seventeen new buildings were constructed. Murray was also involved with the National Science Foundation during his presidency, which brought national recognition to Texas Tech.

After leaving the presidency, he continued to teach geology. Nancy died following a stroke after 40-plus years of marriage. Murray later met and married fellow geologist Sally Marie Williams. Murray left his stamp on Texas Tech, but also, literally, on the planet. A seafloor structure in the Gulf of Mexico is known as the Murray Basin, and there's the Murray Foreland in Antarctica. Murray felt his most important impact, however, was that left on the scientists, administrators, and teachers he launched in his many roles at LSU and Texas Tech.

Photograph of students attending an event in May 1967 concerning changing the name of Texas Technological College to Texas State University or Texas Tech University. Murray is standing at the podium addressing those in attendance.

Given the arid climate of West Texas, Murray started the International Center for Arid and Semiarid Land Studies, which has gone on to partner with institutions around the world in other arid environments.

Janet Perez

Janet Perez was in Spain on a Fulbright scholarship when she started interviewing contemporary Spanish novelists. "At the time, very little was known about recent [postwar] literature in Spain, so upon return I found myself in demand as a lecturer, as well as able to publish basically whatever I wrote," wrote Perez in the 2012 fall newsletter for Texas Tech's Department of Classical & Modern Languages and Literatures (CMLL). Perez retired the following year and died in 2016. She had spent her life pursuing her interests and helping others find a path to pursue theirs.

Her accomplishments, honors and awards make a long and impressive list. The "abbreviated" resume of this woman from the Ozarks—who edited her high school yearbook and wrote pieces for her church and school newspaper—ran seventy pages. To highlight some of the accomplishments from that lengthy list:

- Horn Professor of Romance Languages in 1989.
- Editor of *Hispania*, the scholarly journal of the American Association of Teachers of Spanish and Portuguese.
- Member of the North American Academy of the Spanish Language.
- Corresponding Member of the Spanish Royal Academy of Letters.
- The Order of Don Quixote.
- Honorary Fellow of the Hispanic Society of America, a worldwide group limited to 400 members.
- Co-editor of the *Monographic Review/Revista monografica*, with her husband.
- Assistant Dean of Texas Tech's Graduate School from 1985 to 2000.
- More than 250 articles and chapters in books; more than 300 entries in reference works; and more than 220 professional paper presentations and invited lectures.

Her husband Genaro—also on Tech's CMLL faculty—said Perez would say her best achievement was "helping other women finish their dissertations and get on with their lives and not have to depend on men." She hooded dozens of PhDs. Like many women of her generation, Perez was a trailblazer who had to deal with roadblocks her male colleagues didn't face.

Before coming to Lubbock in the late '70s, Perez was at the University of North Carolina, where she was the first woman hired full time in the school's Department of Romance Languages. When she came up for promotion—already with a few books published—she was passed over; a man got the promotion. She was planning to sue the university but didn't and was promoted the next year. "I'm the first person I ever heard of who had to obtain tenure three times because before Affirmative Action skullduggery was rampant," she wrote in 2012. Perez eventually became the first Affirmative Action officer for her department.

Perez was also sexually harassed while at North Carolina, said her husband. "She saw how difficult it was for women," he said. So she helped, referring to herself as a "compulsive mentor." Both Perez and her husband admired Spanish writers such as Gonzalo Torrente Ballester and Ana María Matute. She wrote books on both and others among her many published works. "She was a wonderful woman," said Genaro. He was teaching at the University of Texas Permian Basin and had heard of her, then saw her at conferences. They met at a conference in Baton Rouge, and he asked her what she was working on. "Silence," she said. They clicked. She offered to get him some books based on their chat. Two years later they were married.

Image courtesy of Genaro Perez

The "abbreviated" resume of this woman from the Ozarks ran seventy pages.

James Reckner

Originally from Philadelphia, James Reckner at the age of eighteen joined the United States Navy in 1958. His service took him into the Pacific, where he met his wife Middy in New Zealand. He became an officer and served two tours of duty in the Vietnam War, the first in 1963 to evacuate Americans if needed. A second came from 1968 to 1971 as an adviser to the Vietnamese naval river assault group. Those experiences became a major influence in his life.

Following his retirement from naval service, he studied at the University of Auckland, which led to a PhD in history. Texas Tech University offered him a position in 1988 as a history professor, where for two decades he taught courses and wrote about US naval history. During that time, he found that veterans of the Vietnam conflict felt no one seemed to care about their service or the outcome of that war. The university library had no books on the topic. As a result, he made his most lasting contribution to the university and to history by establishing the Vietnam Center and Archive in 1989 to encourage careful study of that conflict and the United States's role in it.

The Center brought to the university leading figures in government and the military from the wartime period. Reckner and the Center received both recognition and awards. The Vietnam Archive has come to include over 20 million pages in the form of manuscripts, documents, photographs, slides, artifacts, maps, films, recordings, and oral histories. Thus, it claims to be second only to the US National Archives as a collection on this topic. The Center also hosts conferences and lectures. Reckner explained that the center and archive provide information on a range of views and memories of the Vietnam War, including those of Americans who opposed the war as well as veterans who served there.

Reckner visited Vietnam in 1998 for the first time since the end of the conflict. He attended a conference and met the North Vietnamese army commander. Beyond the role of the archive, the Vietnam Center at Texas Tech has developed scholarships for students in Vietnam and Cambodia that make it possible for them to attend college. Some American veterans of the conflict have organized efforts through the Vietnam Center to provide medical equipment for hospitals in Vietnam and books for libraries there. The Center also organizes trips for graduate students to visit Vietnam and see battlefields as well as religious and archeological sites. Reckner's efforts have led to a wide range of positive academic and humanitarian results.

James Reckner died on November 16, 2018. His obituary recognized that he "lived his life as a great adventure shaped by duty and graced with joy."

Reckner's efforts have led to a wide range of positive academic and humanitarian results.

Henry Shine

Texas Tech was established on February 10, 1923—thirty-eight days after Henry Shine was born in London. A little more than three decades later the man and the institution met. Shine found a home to teach and conduct research to fulfill his passion of unwrapping chemical mysteries. Along the way, Tech's chemistry department became world renowned. As a case in point, after Shine spoke at Montreal's McGill University in 1968, he received a letter. A snippet read: *In most ways it was the best (lecture) of the year and if lingering doubts existed hereabouts on the depth and quality of chemical research in West Texas, you have dispelled these totally.*

After Shine finished school in London, he started working as a bookkeeper for Warner Bros. First National studios. When World War II began in 1939, his family moved to Sunbury-on-Thames, thirteen miles southwest of central London, to escape German bombing raids. Shine did not want to commute to London and got a job as a laboratory assistant, because he'd done chemistry in school. That led to an industrial chemistry job for a soap company when he got his "call up" papers for military service. Shine asked for a six-month deferral so he could continue his college classes at night. "I waited outside while this body of august-looking men . . . discussed my case," said Shine in a 2021 interview at his Lubbock home.

They told him he could have a two-year deferment if he would go to the University of London full time for a chemistry degree. He ended up on the west coast of Wales, where the university had relocated because of the war. Shine was pleasantly surprised. He thought college students all had full-time jobs and went to school at night like he did. He focused on chemistry and physics. After college he took a job but was bored with the work and found a post doing research with a professor at Bedford College. Shine was asked to find out what made up German jet fuels, a process called Grignard reactions. Shine came to America to further study the mechanism. After learning and trying out an industry job and disliking it, he interviewed for a position at Texas Tech.

Shine was sold on the vision of Joe Dennis, head of Tech's chemistry department, of building a research and graduate department along with undergraduate teaching. He'd never heard of Lubbock and had to find an atlas to see where he and his wife Sellie were moving.

He could also pursue his research as a mechanistic organic chemist. Shine discovered how the benzidine rearrangement took place, which had been an enigma for a century. That work helped synthetic organic chemists develop new processes. Between his teaching load and quest to unlock chemistry riddles, Shine returned to his lab many times after dinner and spent some Saturdays reading journals in the school library. He was Tech's first Horn Professor in chemistry and won numerous university awards. His research work was supported by the National Science Foundation, the Air Force Office of Scientific Research, and the Robert A. Welch Foundation. A prominent lecture series now bears the name Henry J. Shine.

When the Shines, both born Jewish, moved to Lubbock in 1954, they were not very religious, but in their new home they decided to become more involved with Judaism. Daughter Stephanie became president of Lubbock's synagogue, Congregation Shaareth Israel. She's also the Executive Director of the Texas Tech University Center for Early Head Start in the department of Human Development and Family Sciences.

Images courtesy of the Southwest Collection / Special Collections Library

Mary Jeanne van Appledorn, Lawrence Graves, and Shine. Dr. Graves was also a university administrator who served as interim president of Texas Tech in 1979. Drs. van Appledorn and Shine were both Horn Professors.

Shine discovered how the benzidine rearrangement took place, which had been an enigma for a century.

Jennifer Smith

Jennifer Smith's dream job was DNA forensic analyst, but she only lasted six months in that role. Getting yelled at and cussed out by police and lawyers and writing reports for the FBI ruined the dream.

Then there was the nightmare-like smell. "TV glamorizes the whole CSI thing. They don't talk about the smell—bleach and death; it's a smell you don't forget," said Smith, sitting in her office in the Department of Biological Sciences greenhouse just south of the Biology building.

Smith is greenhouse manager, along with teaching and doing research. It's a much better environment for her nose. "When people say 'stop and smell the roses,' I'm the one stopping and smelling the pine tree in the hallway because it smells like the forest," said Smith, who also loves the smell of wet dirt when the greenhouse is watered. "I can smell wet dirt all day—which probably sounds weird to a normal person," she said.

Once Smith decided to walk away from death's stench, she returned to the world of plants. The Lubbock native got her bachelor's in biology at Texas Tech, then added a master's in crop sciences before trying to solve crimes. She came back to Texas Tech to get her doctorate, planting herself in a new career in a place where biology helps the world. Years before that, though, Smith took an aptitude test after high school that indicated that her top proclivity was nut gatherer. "My family and I all laughed like that is the most ridiculous thing I've ever heard," she said. But her first job out of high school was in a peanut lab, crushing peanuts to test the oil for fatty acid content. "So I ran back to my parents and said, 'Does this make me a nut gatherer'?" she said.

Now she works in a place where research is done on cotton, grapevines, sorghum—and peanuts. Most of the research is on cotton, with Texas Tech planted in the middle of the massive West Texas cotton patch. Smith takes genes from a creosote bush or desert shrub and puts them inside cotton, which will hopefully help it be more drought tolerant. As the Ogallala Aquifer—from where West Texas gets it irrigation water—starts to dry up, finding ways to create cotton that can thrive on less water is vital. The greenhouses have growth chambers where researchers can turn up the heat, create day/night settings, and adjust carbon dioxide. Other research is done in fields. Then there are plants used for teaching non-majors and majors.

Smith's greenhouse is one of a few on campus. The best-known one is the Horticulture Gardens and Greenhouse Complex just north of United Supermarkets Arena where plants used around campus are grown. People who do work in her greenhouse take what they learn around the world, Smith said. She's still in touch with a former Red Raider from Africa who came to learn how to attack a parasite. He also took peanut breeding technology he learned at Texas Tech to start peanut production. Another study found that fish excrete a chemical hormone that kills mosquito larvae but not other aquatic life. A product to kill mosquitoes in rice paddy fields to protect workers was then created. Smith also studies how plants react to different environments. "I have a plant here and a clone at home. The flowers on the one in the greenhouse are white and the one at my home is pink," she said, wanting to delve deeper to understand why.

Images courtesy of Jennifer Smith

Smith's greenhouse is one of a few on campus. The best-known one is the Horticulture Gardens and Greenhouse Complex just north of United Supermarkets Arena where plants used around campus are grown.

Jane Winer

Jane Winer lived an interesting life even before she came to Texas Tech University. Her father was an infantry officer in the Pacific Theater of WWII where he lost his right eye. After the war, he joined the new foreign aid program of the US Department of State, serving in Iran, Nepal, and Vietnam. Her mother taught school, established libraries, and served as a principal in Iran and Nepal.

Winer attended the Presbyterian Mission School and the American Dependents School in Tehran, Iran, through the 5th grade. She started 6th grade at the Albion Grammar School in New York but finished 6th through 11th grades studying at Lincoln School, Kathmandu, Nepal, and University of Nebraska correspondence courses. She graduated from George Mason Junior-Senior High School in Falls Church, Virginia, and went to college at State University of New York at Albany.

She arrived at Texas Tech University in 1975 as a beginning assistant professor immediately after receiving her PhD from Ohio State. Thirty-five years later, she retired from Tech as a tenured full professor and dean emerita. She directed the counseling psychology doctoral training program for three years and served as associate dean for research in the College of Arts & Sciences for four. Winer rose to become dean of the College of Arts & Sciences, the largest college on campus, for seventeen years. She helped bring a Phi Beta Kappa chapter to Texas Tech and supported the departure of the fine arts and mass communications departments from the College of Arts & Sciences to develop their own colleges. She helped establish the Honors College and buttressed founding dean Gary Bell at every turn.

Ultimately, she became interim provost and vice president for academic affairs and finished her career as special assistant to the president. Recommending her appointment as Dean Emerita, President Guy Bailey told the Board of Regents that Winer was perhaps the longest-serving dean of a large arts and sciences college in a research university in the country. The Honors College named the Winer House for her, with its central virtue being courage.

Early in her time in Lubbock, she married Dr. Monty Strauss, professor of mathematics, who served as senior associate dean of the Graduate School and wrote a college calculus book. Both served the Congregation Shaareth Israel of Lubbock in various capacities and worked to develop a Jewish Archive at the Southwest Collection / Special Collections Library at Tech, as well as supported numerous scholarships and endowments benefiting students and the university. Ten years after retirement, illness prompted a move nearer Monty's family in the Dallas area, but the couple maintain deep ties to Lubbock and Tech.

Winer's early privileged life, even as she was often surrounded by poverty, disease, and violence, instilled in her a lifelong sense of responsibility to create circumstances for others to succeed. She applied those principles throughout her career, making Texas Tech a better place for generations of students, staff, and faculty to thrive, and improved the world from her island of enlightenment on the Llano Estacado.

Photo by Rhonda Cummings

Winer arrived at Texas Tech University in 1975 as a beginning assistant professor immediately after receiving her PhD from Ohio State. Thirty-five years later, she retired from Tech as a tenured full professor and dean emerita.

The Honors College named the Winer House for her, with its central virtue being courage.

Index

Note: Entry numbers in italics refer to images.